25 Business Skills

in English

Mark McCracken

DELTA PUBLISHING COMPANY
A DIVISION OF DELTA SYSTEMS COMPANY, INC.

1400 Miller Parkway
McHenry, IL 60050 USA
(815) 363–3582   Toll Free (800) 323–8270
www.delta–systems.com

Printed in the United States of America

10 9 8 7 6 5 4 3 2

Author: Mark McCracken

Design/Page Layout: Treasure Tomal

ISBN 1–887744–85–1

Table of Contents

Skill 1: Control a conversation

Skill 1:
Control a conversation

 GOALS:
Be aggressive. Speak loudly. Speak quickly. Memorize the phrases. Interrupt the speaker if you don't understand. Ask the speaker to continue after you get the information that you need. Make sure you understand the information correctly. Use the phrases as quickly in English as you can in your own language. Control a conversation using only your voice, without using your hands or eye contact.

BENEFITS:
By controlling a conversation, you can eliminate miscommunication errors. You can control how fast the other person speaks. You can force the other person to explain the meaning of words you don't understand. You make the other person responsible for explaining everything clearly to you.

Phrases:

Excuse me.

Could you say that again?

Could you say that again more slowly?

Could you say that again more loudly?

Could you say that again more clearly?

Could you say that again from the beginning?

What did you say after ___?

What did you say before ___?

What does ___ mean?

How do you say ___ in English?

How do you say ___ in Japanese?

How do you spell ____?

___ is spelled _____.

How do you pronounce _____?

A: Let me make sure I understand.
    You said "____." Is that correct?

B: Yes, that's correct. / No, that isn't correct.

Please continue.

PERFORMANCE 1.1 - STUDENT A

 Work with a partner. Read sentences 1-4 to your partner. Sometimes read the phrases unclearly, too quickly or too softly. In sentences 5-8, write down what your partner says. Control the conversation to get all the information correctly.

1. At least five people were killed on Friday when an AirMundovia DC-9 carrying 78 people plowed into houses and vehicles in heavy rain after careening off the runway in northern Chile, an airline official said.

2. A powerful 8.5-magnitude earthquake jolted Japan's hilly northeast Sunday, injuring at least 96 people and damaging more than 1,600 homes.

3. A series of bomb blasts struck two southern German towns within minutes of each other Saturday, killing over a dozen people and wounding many more, officials said.

4. The Dow Jones industrials ended down 128.98 points, 1.20 percent, at 10,597.86 with the tech-heavy Nasdaq slumping 117.28 points, 3.20 percent, at 3,365.02.

5. _____

_____

_____

6. _____

_____

_____

7. _____

_____

_____

8. _____

_____

_____

PERFORMANCE 1.1 – STUDENT B

Work with a partner. In sentences 1-4, write down what your partner says. Control the conversation to get all the information correctly. Read sentences 5-8 to your partner. Sometimes read the phrases unclearly, too quickly or too softly.

1. _____

   _____

   _____

2. _____

   _____

   _____

3. _____

   _____

   _____

4. _____

   _____

   _____

5. The U.S. Army Thursday awarded Jolly Data Corporation a huge contract for data services in a deal that could be worth more than $8 billion and change the face of government computing.

6. Internet service LearnEnglishNow.com on Monday said its auditors have questioned whether it can continue as a going concern, adding its name to the list of web companies with financial troubles.

7. The space shuttle Discovery should be ready for launch on Tuesday, as soon as a NASA crew can take some fuel out of the shuttle's booster rockets, officials said on Monday.

8. Babies who are born about 3 months premature are several times more likely to have problems in school than children born at full-term, results of a study suggest.

PERFORMANCE 1.2 – STUDENT A

Work with a partner. Read sentences 1, 3, 5 and 7 to your partner. Sometimes read the phrases unclearly, too quickly or too softly. In sentences 2, 4, 6 and 8, write down what your partner says. Control the conversation to get all the information correctly.

1. Mr. Kevin James, the famous business professor from Bradley University, will be speaking at a banquet on Friday, November 17th, at 6:35 p.m., in the Olympic Ballroom.

2. _____

   _____

   _____

3. The space shuttle Discovery and its six crew members are back in Florida because computer problems forced NASA to bring the shuttle home early after just three days in orbit.

4. _____

   _____

   _____

5. Bank account number 19385667AD7, belonging to Mr. Thomas Shillington, contains $75.

6. _____

   _____

   _____

7. Please send the package to Bill Mustang, Apartment 295-B, 4863 East Terrace Drive, St. Augustine, South Carolina 79346, USA.

8. _____

   _____

   _____

PERFORMANCE 1.2 - STUDENT B

***Work with a partner. In sentences 1, 3, 5 and 7, write down what your partner says.
Control the conversation to get all the information correctly. Read sentences 2, 4, 6
and 8 to your partner. Sometimes read the phrases unclearly, too quickly or too softly.***

1. _____

   _____

   _____

2. Miss Sandy Carlson, of Allison Travel, wants to meet with you at the Springfield Sunshine Inn Hotel, on Friday, March 30th, at 2:35 p.m., to discuss preparations for your trip to the Grand Canyon.

3. _____

   _____

   _____

4. The Irish Republican Army has claimed responsibility for a bomb hoax that disrupted the Eastern Florida Soccer Championships and led police to evacuate 900 fans on Sunday.

5. _____

   _____

   _____

6. There is $97 in account number 3867FRJ, which is registered to Mr. John Williams of Palmdale, Illinois.

7. _____

   _____

   _____

8. You received a registered letter from Edith Ruby, who lives in Apartment 354-C, 3963 South Bottom Road, Defiance, Florida 57438, USA.

PERFORMANCE 1.3 – STUDENT A

Work with a partner. Read sentences 1, 3, 5, and 7 to your partner. Sometimes read the phrases unclearly, too quickly or too softly. In sentences 2, 4, 6, and 8 write down what your partner says. Control the conversation to get all the information correctly.

1. Bumbleton Products Company sells a wide range of consumer products worldwide in six business segments: laundry and cleaning, paper, beauty care, food and beverage, health care, and accessories.

2. _____

_____

_____

3. Speedy Motors Corporation manufactures and sells cars, trucks, boats, related parts and accessories. Speedy Financial Services offers financing, insurance, and vehicle and equipment leasing.

4. _____

_____

_____

5. National Telephone offers voice, data and video telecommunications services, including cellular telephone and internet services, to businesses, consumers and government agencies.

6. _____

_____

_____

7. Software Unlimited Company creates, manufactures, supports and licenses a wide range of software products, including scalable operating systems, server applications, software development tools, and worker productivity applications.

8. _____

_____

_____

PERFORMANCE 1.3 – STUDENT B

Work with a partner. In sentences 1, 3, 5, and 7, write down what your partner says. Control the conversation to get all the information correctly. Read sentences 2, 4, 6, and 8 to your partner. Sometimes read the phrases unclearly, too quickly or too softly.

1. _____
   _____
   _____

2. Baxter Motors Corporation designs, manufactures and markets automobiles, trucks, airplanes and related parts, designs and manufactures locomotives and heavy-duty transmissions, and manages an insurance company.

3. _____
   _____
   _____

4. Brown Grain Company manufactures, markets and distributes a wide variety of ready-to-eat cereal and other grain-based convenience food breakfast products worldwide.

5. _____
   _____
   _____

6. Red Ink Finance is a diversified holding company whose businesses offer a wide range of financial services, including banking, insurance, mortgage and investment services to consumers and corporate customers around the world.

7. _____
   _____
   _____

8. Superior Market Company is a multi-line retailer that provides a wide array of merchandise and services through retail, service, credit, insurance, and international segments.

Skill 1:
Control a conversation

EVALUATION

☐ I speak loudly.

☐ I can speak quickly.

☐ I am aggressive.

☐ I interrupt as soon as I don't understand.

☐ I have memorized the phrases needed to control a conversation.

☐ I can use the phrases in English as quickly as in my own language.

☐ After I write something down, I can check to make sure I wrote it correctly.

☐ I can control a conversation without using my hands, eye contact, or facial expressions.

☐ If someone is speaking too quickly, I am able to make him or her speak at a speed that I can understand.

☐ If I don't understand the meaning of a word someone uses, I can make the other person explain the meaning clearly.

☐ I have the confidence needed to use the phrases in real life with native English speakers.

Skill 2: Start a conversation

Skill 2:
Start a conversation

GOALS:
Stand up. Introduce yourself to someone you have never met. Look the other person in the eye when you talk to them. Appear confident. Shake hands firmly. Smile.

BENEFITS:
You must meet people in order to do business. By starting a conversation and appearing interested, it will be more likely that the other person will buy your product or service.

Conversation:

A: Hello, my name is _____.
   (shake hands)
B: My name is _____.

A: It's nice to meet you.
B: It's nice to meet you too.

A: Who do you work for?
B: I work for _____.
   (company name)

A: What do you do?
B: I'm a _____.
   (engineer, teacher, manager, executive assistant)

A: Where do you live?
B: I live in _____. (city name)

A: Do you have a family?
B: Yes, there are _____ people in my family:
   my wife, my daughter and I.

A: What do you like to do in your free time?
B: I like _____.
   (playing tennis, reading, watching TV)

A: Well, it was nice meeting you. (shake hands)
B: It was nice meeting you too.

A: Good-bye.
B: Good-bye.

PERFORMANCE 2.1

Practice the conversation (refer to page 11) word for word with every student in the class. Take turns being A and B.

PERFORMANCE 2.2

Practice the conversation again word for word with every student in the class. Take turns being A and B. This time, however, B must speak from memory.

PERFORMANCE 2.3

Practice the conversation again word for word with every student in the class. Take turns being A and B. This time, however, both A and B must speak from memory.

PERFORMANCE 2.4

Practice the conversation again, from memory, but this time B should use the phrases "And you?" and "How about you?" after giving each answer.

PERFORMANCE 2.5

Practice the conversation with every student in the class. Take turns being A and B. This time, ask follow-up questions, like "How old is your daughter?" or "What TV shows do you like to watch?" to make the conversation more interesting.

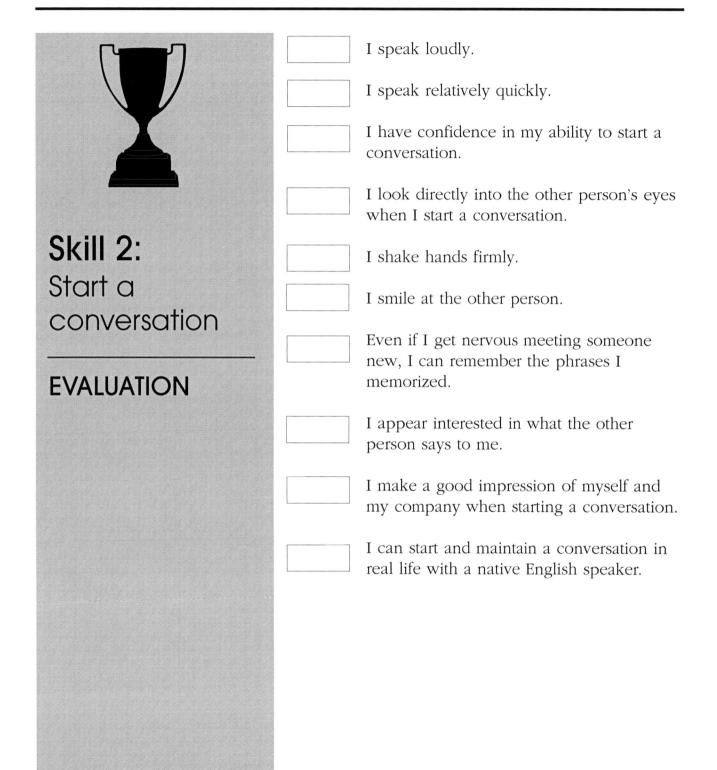

Skill 2:
Start a conversation

EVALUATION

☐ I speak loudly.

☐ I speak relatively quickly.

☐ I have confidence in my ability to start a conversation.

☐ I look directly into the other person's eyes when I start a conversation.

☐ I shake hands firmly.

☐ I smile at the other person.

☐ Even if I get nervous meeting someone new, I can remember the phrases I memorized.

☐ I appear interested in what the other person says to me.

☐ I make a good impression of myself and my company when starting a conversation.

☐ I can start and maintain a conversation in real life with a native English speaker.

Skill 3: Introduce yourself

Skill 3:
Introduce yourself

GOALS:
Stand up. Introduce yourself to a large group of people. Talk about your background. Talk about your current job. Talk a little about your personal life. Memorize your introduction. Make eye contact with everyone in the room. Be energetic. Speak clearly. Speak loudly. Speak without hesitation. Smile.

BENEFITS:
People are more likely to speak to you and work effectively with you if they have a basic understanding of who you are and what your abilities are. People will become accustomed to your accent. You will probably feel more comfortable participating in group discussions if you have already given a short introductory speech.

Phrases:

My name is _____.

I work for _____.

I'm a _____.

I live in _____.

There are ___ people in my family: my _____ and I.

I like _____ in my free time.

PERFORMANCE 3.1

Using some of the phrases on page 15, write your self-introduction below. Your teacher will help you. When you are finished, your teacher will correct any mistakes you have made. Next, practice reading the speech to yourself about 20 times. When it is memorized, give your speech to the entire class.

Skill 3:
Introduce yourself

EVALUATION

☐ I speak loudly.

☐ I can introduce myself at the same speaking speed as native English speakers.

☐ I can give my self-introduction speech to the class anytime the teacher asks me to.

☐ I am confident about giving the speech to people I have never met before.

☐ I don't worry about having to give a short self-introduction speech.

☐ Six months from now, my speech will still be in my memory.

☐ I make eye contact with everyone in the room.

☐ I am energetic when I give my speech.

Skill 4: Describe your job and your company

Skill 4:
Describe your job and your company

GOALS:
Clearly and accurately explain your company's history and the products and services your company offers. Give some basic financial information. Describe in detail exactly what you do for the company.

BENEFITS:
Customers and business associates are more likely to work with your company, and you, if they have a clear understanding of your company and your role at the company.

PERFORMANCE 4.1

The words in each sentence are not in the correct order. Rewrite each sentence, putting the words in the correct order.

established Company in Nakano was Cosmetics 1976.

1. _____

_____

shadow produces lipstick eye and mascara it.

2. _____

_____

customers Japanese women its are main business.

3. _____

_____

office Nara its head in located is Japan.

4. _____

_____

Japan factories in has it five.

5. _____

_____

in has it one China factory.

6. _____

_____

384 has it employees.

7. _____

_____

in twenty-three head work its office people.

8. _____

_____

president Mary its Nakano is.

9. _____

_____

500,000,000 sales its 1999 in were Japanese about yen annual.

10. _____

_____

PERFORMANCE 4.2

Write the questions that match the answers in Performance 4.1. Use the words 'your company' in each sentence.

1. _____

   _____

2. _____

   _____

3. _____

   _____

4. _____

   _____

5. _____

   _____

6. _____

   _____

7. _____

   _____

8. _____

   _____

9. _____

   _____

10. _____

    _____

PERFORMANCE 4.3

Write the answers to the questions in Performance 4.2. Use the name of the company you work for in each of your answers.

1. _____

_____

2. _____

_____

3. _____

_____

4. _____

_____

5. _____

_____

6. _____

_____

7. _____

_____

8. _____

_____

9. _____

_____

10. _____

_____

PERFORMANCE 4.4

Exchange books with your partner. Give your partner Performance 4.3. Your partner will ask you the questions from Performance 4.2. From memory, answer the questions clearly and confidently. Take turns.

PERFORMANCE 4.5

Rewrite each sentence, putting the words in the correct order.

established was Burke Products 1965 in.

1. _____

   _____

produces small gasoline engines and it pumps.

2. _____

   _____

customers are main its factories large.

3. _____

   _____

head is its Cincinnati, Ohio in located office.

4. _____

   _____

in factories six country this has it.

5. _____

_____

offices seven has countries other in it.

6. _____

_____

employees 5,850 has it.

7. _____

_____

people office fifty in head its work.

8. _____

_____

James Burke president its is.

9. _____

_____

1999 about were its sales annual $1,000,000,000 in

10. _____

_____

PERFORMANCE 4.6

From memory, write the questions that match the answers in Performance 4.5.
Use the words 'your company' in each sentence. Do not look at Performance 4.2

1. _____

   _____

2. _____

   _____

3. _____

   _____

4. _____

   _____

5. _____

   _____

6. _____

   _____

7. _____

   _____

8. _____

   _____

9. _____

   _____

10. _____

    _____

PERFORMANCE 4.7

From memory, write the answers to the questions in Performance 4.6. Use the name of the company you work for in each of your answers. Do not look at Performance 4.3.

1. _____

2. _____

3. _____

4. _____

5. _____

6. _____

7. _____

8. _____

9. _____

10. _____

PERFORMANCE 4.8

Memorize the questions and answers in Performance 4.6 and 4.7. Ask and answer the questions with all the other people in your class.

PERFORMANCE 4.9

Write a detailed description of your job. Use the phrases to help you. After you are finished, your teacher will correct any mistakes you may have made. Next, memorize the sentences.

I work for _____.
I work in the _____ department.
I am responsible for _____.

_____

_____

_____

_____

PERFORMANCE 4.10

From memory, have the following conversation with the other people in your class.

A: What do you do?
B: (your job description)

PERFORMANCE 4.11

Combine starting a conversation with describing your job and company. From memory, start a conversation. Then ask and answer questions about your job and company. Try to make a natural conversation and use all the phrases you have learned.

Skill 4:
Describe your job and your company

___

EVALUATION

☐ From memory, I can clearly and accurately answer the 10 questions about my company.

☐ If I met a native speaker today, I would feel confident in using the questions to learn about the other person's company.

☐ I have memorized a complete description of what I do in my job.

☐ Next month, I will still be able to give someone an accurate description of my job anytime without having to look at my notes.

Skill 5: Use large and small numbers

Skill 5:
Use large and small numbers

GOALS:
You should be able to quickly, confidently and accurately read numbers out loud. When you hear a native English speaker use numbers in a natural way, you should be able to write the numbers down as quickly as you hear them. You should be able to add, subtract, multiply and divide in English.

BENEFITS:
Numbers are used to measure productivity, value and wealth. You will be able to exchange data with a native English speaker.

Conversations:

A: How much were your annual sales?
B: Our annual sales were _____.

A: How much were your total expenses?
B: Our total expenses were _____.

A: How much was your gross profit?
B: Our gross profit was _____.

A: How much was your profit margin?
B: Our profit margin was _____.

A: How many employees does your company have?
B: Our company has _____ employees.

How much is one plus one?
1 + 1 = 2   One plus one equals two.

How much is three minus one?
3 – 1 = 2   Three minus one equals two.

How much is six divided by three?
6 ÷ 3 = 2   Six divided by three equals two.

How much is three times three?
3 X 3 = 9   Three times three equals nine.

Notes:

annual sales	= the total revenue or turnover from your business
total expenses	= all costs including the cost of goods sold, overhead, labor, etc.
gross profit	= annual sales – total expenses
profit margin	= gross profit / annual sales
123,456,789,312	= one hundred twenty–three billion, four hundred fifty–six million, seven hundred eighty–nine thousand, three hundred twelve
0.000536%	= zero point zero zero zero five three six percent

PERFORMANCE 5.1 – STUDENT A

 Work with a partner. Using the phrases below, ask for information about 1, 3, 5, 7, 9. You will ask five questions for each. Write down what your partner says. In 2, 4, 6, 8, 10, answer your partner's questions using the numbers. Check your answers.

annual sales
total expenses
gross profit
profit margin
number of employees

1.		2.	439,297,317,270 euros 346,065,468,347 euros 93,231,848,923 euros 21.22% 28,395
3.		4.	97,419,790 dollars 87,496,803 dollars 9,922,987 dollars 10.185% 492
5.		6.	93,960,316,000 won 83,560,054,000 won 10,370,262,000 won 11.0368% 45,035
7.		8.	84,003,057 pounds 83,950,915 pounds 52,142 pounds 0.0620% 13,357
9.		10.	9,390,219,500 yen 8,239,257,400 yen 1,150,962,100 yen 12.25% 33,564

PERFORMANCE 5.1 – STUDENT B

 Work with a partner. In 1, 3, 5, 7, 9, answer your partner's questions using the numbers. Using the phrases below, ask for information about 2, 4, 6, 8, 10. You will ask five questions for each. Write down what your partner says. Check your answers.

annual sales
total expenses
gross profit
profit margin
number of employees

1. 124,715,845,850 yen 120,046,362,686 yen 4,669,483,164 yen 3.74% 19,396	2.
3. 21,848,437 dollars 14,413,030 dollars 7,435,407 dollars 34.031% 210	4.
5. 79,597,047,000 euros 63,914,540,000 euros 15,682,507,000 euros 19.702% 12,508	6.
7. 45,416,260 pounds 36,794,035 pounds 8,622,225 pounds 18.98% 354	8.
9. 2,496,935,000 yen 1,917,970,000 yen 578,965,000 yen 23.187% 78,395	10.

PERFORMANCE 5.2 – STUDENT A

 Work with a partner. In problems 1, 3, 5 answer your partner's questions. In problems 2, 4, 6 ask your partner for the answers. Check your answers.

1. 12 + 65 = 77
    19 + 35 = 54
    392 – 23 = 369
    59 – 12 = 47
    64 ÷ 8 = 8
    79 ÷ 3.2 = 24.6875
    6 X 2.3 = 13.8
    8 X 21 = 168

2. 658 + 95 =
    97 + 458 =
    956 – 236 =
    826 – 412 =
    927 ÷ 3 =
    592 ÷ 0.25 =
    8.15 X 623 =
    9 X 194 =

3. 587,456,345,234 + 254,875,548,021 = 842,331,893,255
    78,054,264 – 54,089,978 =23,964,286
    256,902,446 ÷ 638 = 402,668.4107
    346,092,298 X 210 = 72,679,382,580

4. 209,596,238,018 + 390,592,621,235 =
    983,378,897,247 – 389,129,373,845 =
    543,845,209,398 ÷ 34,526,745 =
    764,346,745 X 16 =

5. 366,781,548,016 + 456,971,468,567 = 823,753,016,583
    164,684,247,681– 87,570,045,060 = 77,114,202,621
    839,369,209,346 ÷ 298.1543 = 2,815,217,521.0822
    0.003526 X 28,569,329 = 100,735.4541

6. 435,785,671,054 + 248,546,180,481 =
    914,456,321,645 – 456,871,458,461 =
    0.004785 ÷ 0.002334 =
    987,465 X 124.28397 =

PERFORMANCE 5.2 – STUDENT B

Work with a partner. In problems 1, 3, 5 ask your partner for the answers. In problems 2, 4, 6 answer your partner's questions.

1. $12 + 65 =$
    $19 + 35 =$
    $392 - 23 =$
    $59 - 12 =$
    $64 \div 8 =$
    $79 \div 3.2 =$
    $6 \times 2.3 =$
    $8 \times 21 =$

2. $658 + 95 = 753$
    $97 + 458 = 555$
    $956 - 236 = 720$
    $826 - 412 = 414$
    $927 \div 3 = 309$
    $592 \div 0.25 = 2368$
    $8.15 \times 623 = 5,007.45$
    $9 \times 194 = 1746$

3. $587,456,345,234 + 254,875,548,021 =$
    $78,054,264 - 54,089,978 =$
    $256,902,446 \div 638 =$
    $346,092,298 \times 210 =$

4. $209,596,238,018 + 390,592,621,235 = 600,188,859,253$
    $983,378,897,247 - 389,129,373,845 = 594,249,523,402$
    $543,845,209,398 \div 34,526,745 = 15,751.41848$
    $764,346,745 \times 16 = 12,229,547,920$

5. $366,781,548,016 + 456,971,468,567 =$
    $164,684,247,681 - 87,570,045,060 =$
    $839,369,209,346 \div 298.1543 =$
    $0.003526 \times 28,569,329 =$

6. $435,785,671,054 + 248,546,180,481 = 684,331,851,535$
    $914,456,321,645 - 456,871,458,461 = 457,584,863,184$
    $0.004785 \div 0.002334 = 2.0501285$
    $987,465 \times 124.28397 = 122,726,070.4361$

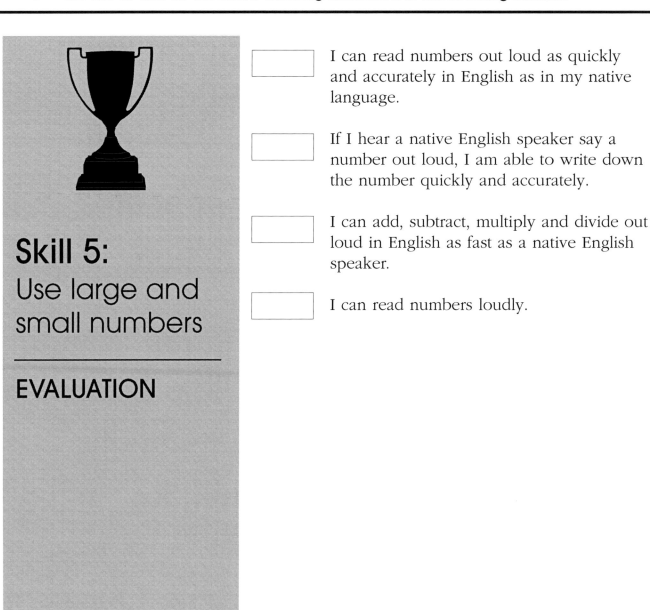

Skill 5:
Use large and small numbers

EVALUATION

☐ I can read numbers out loud as quickly and accurately in English as in my native language.

☐ If I hear a native English speaker say a number out loud, I am able to write down the number quickly and accurately.

☐ I can add, subtract, multiply and divide out loud in English as fast as a native English speaker.

☐ I can read numbers loudly.

Skill 6: Exchange company data

Skill 6:
Exchange company data

 GOALS:
You should be able to use numbers to exchange basic information about various companies. You should be able to exchange addresses, telephone numbers, fax numbers and email addresses.

BENEFITS:
You will be able to ask people how to contact them. You will be able to contact a company by mail, fax, telephone or email.

Memorize the following phrases:

A: Who do you work for?
B: I work for _____.

A: Could I have your address?
B: Our address is _____.

A: Could I have your telephone number?
B: Our telephone number is _____.

A: Could I have your fax number?
B: Our fax number is _____.

A: Could I have your email address?
B: My email address is _____.

A: How many employees does your company have?
B: Our company has _____ employees.

A: Could I have your name?
B: My name is _____.

Notes:

California is abbreviated CA.
(312) 555-1212 =
area code three one two, five five five one two one two

john.smith@LearnEnglishNow.com =
john dot smith at learn English now dot com

PERFORMANCE 6.1 – STUDENT A

Work with a partner. Ask for information about 1, 3, 5, 7, 9. You will ask six questions for each. Write down what your partner says. In 2, 4, 6, 8, 10, answer your partner's questions using the information. Write down what your partner says. Check your answers.

company
address
phone number
fax number
email address
number of employees

1. _____
   _____
   _____
   _____
   _____
   _____

2. O'Neill Park Motors
   2500 O'Neill Park Center
   Phillips, MI 69408
   Phone: (393) 194-5406
   Fax: (393) 149-4806
   Email: opm@oneillpm.com.
   Employees: 349,564

3. _____
   _____
   _____
   _____
   _____
   _____

4. Mizler Trimming Company
   One Mizler Plaza
   P.O. Box 3595
   St. Louis, MO 91973
   Phone: (696) 168-4673
   Fax: (696) 467-2105
   Mizler@mizlertrimming.com
   Employees: 17,051

5. _____
   _____
   _____
   _____
   _____
   _____
   _____

6. Henrich Schlueter Company
   200 East 53rd Street
   Peoria, NY 25430
   Phone: (292) 597-1570
   Fax: (292) 172-2467
   info@HenrichSchlueter.com
   Employees: 469,647

7. _____
   _____
   _____
   _____
   _____
   _____
   _____

8. Marie Pollman Industries
   3456 Wessler Road
   Hoffman Estates, IL 97321
   Phone: (897) 167-2346
   Fax: (897) 469-1560
   MPI@mariepollman.com
   Employees: 497,408

9. _____
   _____
   _____
   _____
   _____
   _____
   _____

10. Alma Metal Industries
    600 Hill Street
    Maple Tree, PA 79019
    Phone: (492) 147-2261
    Fax: (492) 433-5876
    Alma@almametal.com
    Employees: 88,566

PERFORMANCE 6.1 – STUDENT B

Work with a partner. In 1, 3, 5, 7, 9, answer your partner's questions using the information. Ask for information about 2, 4, 6, 8, 10. You will ask six questions for each. Write down what your partner says. Check your answers.

company
address
phone number
fax number
email address
number of employees

1. Green Peach Company
   One Green Peach Plaza
   Springfield, CA 35402
   Phone: (593) 659-1257
   Fax: (593) 894-5436
   Email: shareholders@GreenPeachOnline.com
   Employees: 136,918

2. _____
   _____
   _____
   _____
   _____
   _____

3. East Harper Incorporated
   312 Bernice Avenue
   Scroggins, MI 06548
   Phone: (393) 168-8614
   Fax: (393) 189-5618
   Email: webmaster@EastHarper.com
   Employees: 364,894

4. _____
   _____
   _____
   _____
   _____
   _____

5. Hadams Microdevices
   6486 Avenue of the Americas
   Los Angeles, CA 69761
   Phone: (292) 168-4627
   Fax: (292) 516-4679
   Email: joe.hadams@hadamsmicro.com
   Employees: 187,914

6. _____
   _____
   _____
   _____
   _____
   _____
   _____

7. Red Washborn Company
   One Washborn Drive
   Detroit, MI 61943
   Phone: (495) 648-5160
   Fax: (495) 940-1853
   Email: webmaster@washborn.com
   Employees: 48,561

8. _____
   _____
   _____
   _____
   _____
   _____
   _____

9. North Angelini Industries
   Whittier Tower Building
   Fairmont, AZ 12924
   Phone: (697) 264-8000
   Fax: (697) 125-9840
   Email: jobs@northangelini.com
   Employees: 39,800

10. _____
    _____
    _____
    _____
    _____
    _____
    _____

PERFORMANCE 6.2 – STUDENT A

 Work with a partner. Using the phrases below, ask for information about 1, 3, 5, 7, 9. You will ask six questions for each. Write down what your partner says. In 2, 4, 6, 8, 10, answer your partner's questions using the information. Check your answers.

name
company
head office
company president
telephone number
annual sales

1. _____
   _____
   _____
   _____
   _____
   _____

2. Michael Hightower
   Black Binder Construction
   Williamsburg, Virginia
   Jonathon Rainwater
   998-567-0467
   $267,348,323,906 (1998)

3. _____
   _____
   _____
   _____
   _____
   _____

4. Barry Longsbrough
   Blue House Media Services
   Monroe, South Carolina
   Theodore Shellrather
   592-602-0054
   $227,904 (2002)

5. _____
   _____
   _____
   _____
   _____
   _____

6. Kevin Larson
   Odessa Playtime Limited
   Midland, Texas
   Don Harperland
   698-787-2175
   $254,045,648,015 (2001)

7. _____
   _____
   _____
   _____
   _____
   _____

8. Jill Argon
   Green Burger International
   Southfork, Texas
   Brian Megansworth
   897-457-6448
   $876,456,289,045 (1999)

9. _____
   _____
   _____
   _____
   _____
   _____

10. Gerald Timesworth
    Subbrock Publishing
    Fairfax, Florida
    Lori Phillips
    995-543-0480
    $468,054,016,240 (2000)

PERFORMANCE 6.2 – STUDENT B

 Work with a partner. In 1, 3, 5, 7, 9, answer your partner's questions using the information. Using the phrases below, ask for information about 2, 4, 6, 8, 10. You will ask six questions for each. Write down what your partner says. Check your answers.

name
company
head office
company president
telephone number
annual sales

1. John Williams
   Madison Paints Incorporated
   Peoria, Illinois
   Bill McCormick
   296-365-9875
   $21,406,180 (1999)

2. _____

   _____

   _____

   _____

   _____

   _____

3. Matthew Richards
   Summer Landscaping Company
   Billy Bluff, Arizona
   Tyrone Green
   394-987-6647
   $5,189,017 (2001)

4. _____

   _____

   _____

   _____

   _____

   _____

5. Corrine Ruby
   Publishers Clearance Corporation
   Marilyn Grove, Illinois
   Mary Beth Leuffgen
   708-974-4587
   $100 million (1999)

6. _____
   _____
   _____
   _____
   _____
   _____

7. Richard Eli
   Science Unlimited Company
   Scranton, Iowa
   Edith Scanzoni
   798-658-4724
   $1,257,945 (2000)

8. _____
   _____
   _____
   _____
   _____
   _____

9. Matt Baker
   Clean Living Products Incorporated
   Herring Feather, Wisconsin
   Samuel Douglas
   998-458-4876
   $492,628,945,745 (2002)

10. _____
    _____
    _____
    _____
    _____
    _____

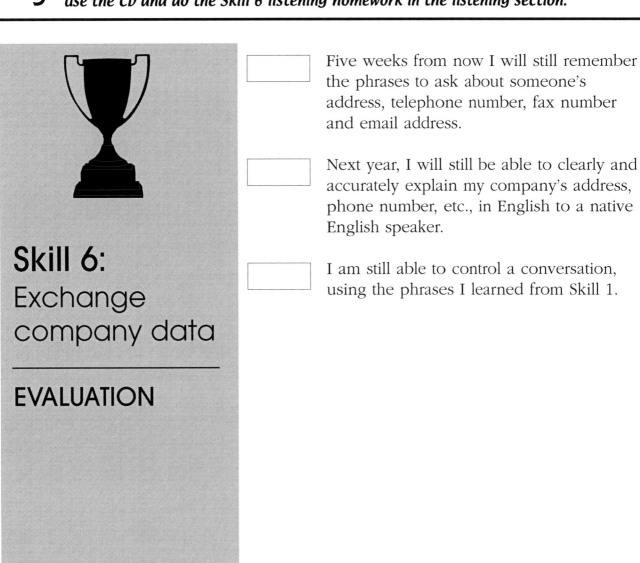

Skill 6:
Exchange company data

EVALUATION

Five weeks from now I will still remember the phrases to ask about someone's address, telephone number, fax number and email address.

Next year, I will still be able to clearly and accurately explain my company's address, phone number, etc., in English to a native English speaker.

I am still able to control a conversation, using the phrases I learned from Skill 1.

Skill 7: Have a job interview

Skill 7:
Have a job interview

GOALS:
Be able to hire new employees, interview for a new job, introduce yourself, and talk about your company.

BENEFITS:
You will be able to go through the job interview process. You will also be better able to hire new employees to help you serve your customers better.

PERFORMANCE 7.1

 Discuss what questions are acceptable and not acceptable in employment interviews in your country, and in your company.

PERFORMANCE 7.2

 In a job interview in the United States, it is against the law to ask questions about race, color, religion, sex, national origin, birthplace, age, physical disability or anything not directly related to the job.

 Read each question and decide if it is probably OK to ask in the United States or not. The answers are at the end of this chapter.

Probably OK	Probably not OK	
( )	( )	Where were you born?
( )	( )	Where were your parents born?
( )	( )	How old are you?
( )	( )	When were you born?
( )	( )	Are you over eighteen years old?
( )	( )	What year did you graduate from high school?
( )	( )	Are you married?
( )	( )	Are you willing to relocate to another city?
( )	( )	Are you engaged?
( )	( )	Do you have any children?
( )	( )	If you get this job, will you be able to take a lot of business trips?
( )	( )	Are you able to lift a twenty-pound box and carry it ten feet?
( )	( )	Which church do you go to?
( )	( )	Do you go to church on Sunday mornings?
( )	( )	Are you available to work on Sunday mornings?
( )	( )	Are you a United States citizen?
( )	( )	What is your nationality?
( )	( )	Are you authorized to work in the U.S.?
( )	( )	Have you ever been arrested?
( )	( )	Have you ever been convicted of a serious crime?
( )	( )	What kind of work does your husband do?
( )	( )	Do you live in an apartment or a house?
( )	( )	How many children do you think you want to have?

PERFORMANCE 7.3 – STUDENT A

Someone will interview to work at your company. Work as a group and write several questions to ask the person. Be sure to include questions about their background.

1. _____
_____

2. _____
_____

3. _____
_____

4. _____
_____

5. _____
_____

6. _____
_____

7. _____
_____

8. _____
_____

9. _____
_____

10. _____
_____

PERFORMANCE 7.3 – STUDENT B

You want to get a new job. Today, you will interview with a new company. Work as a group and write several questions to ask the person who will interview you. Be sure to include questions about all the aspects of the company.

1. _____

   _____

2. _____

   _____

3. _____

   _____

4. _____

   _____

5. _____

   _____

6. _____

   _____

7. _____

   _____

8. _____

   _____

9. _____

   _____

10. _____

   _____

PERFORMANCE 7.4

Work with a partner. Practice a job interview. One person is the interviewer. The other person is the interviewee. Use information about your real company and real life. When you're finished, change roles.

ANSWERS TO PERFORMANCE 7.2

Probably OK	Probably not OK	
( )	(✗)	Where were you born?
( )	(✗)	Where were your parents born?
( )	(✗)	How old are you?
( )	(✗)	When were you born?
(✗)	( )	Are you over eighteen years old?
( )	(✗)	What year did you graduate from high school?
( )	(✗)	Are you married?
(✗)	( )	Are you willing to relocate to another city?
( )	(✗)	Are you engaged?
( )	(✗)	Do you have any children?
(✗)	( )	If you get this job, will you be able to take a lot of business trips?
(✗)	( )	Are you able to lift a twenty-pound box and carry it ten feet?
( )	(✗)	Which church do you go to?
( )	(✗)	Do you go to church on Sunday mornings?
(✗)	( )	Are you available to work on Sunday mornings?
( )	(✗)	Are you a United States citizen?
( )	(✗)	What is your nationality?
(✗)	( )	Are you authorized to work in the U.S.?
( )	(✗)	Have you ever been arrested?
(✗)	( )	Have you ever been convicted of a serious crime?
( )	(✗)	What kind of work does your husband do?
( )	(✗)	Do you live in an apartment or a house?
( )	(✗)	How many children do you think you want to have?

Skill 7:
Have a job interview

EVALUATION

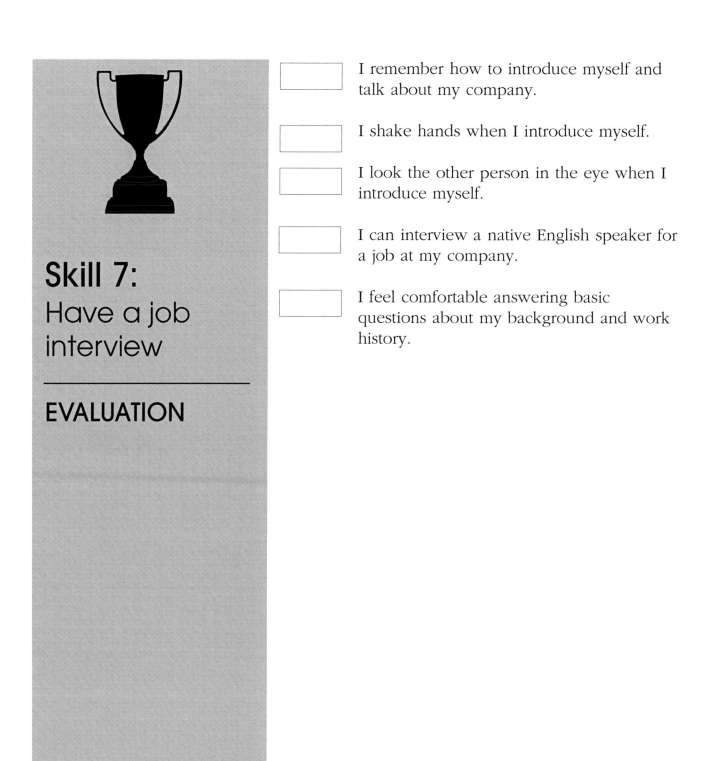

☐ I remember how to introduce myself and talk about my company.

☐ I shake hands when I introduce myself.

☐ I look the other person in the eye when I introduce myself.

☐ I can interview a native English speaker for a job at my company.

☐ I feel comfortable answering basic questions about my background and work history.

Skill 8: Take or leave a telephone message

Skill 8:
Take or leave a telephone message

 GOALS:
When you get a telephone call from an English speaker, you should be able to instantly speak English. Take a telephone message from a native speaker. Speak as fast as a native speaker. Control the conversation. Do not use eye contact or gestures. Check to make sure you wrote the information correctly.

BENEFITS:
You will be able to take a message from a native speaker without getting nervous. You will make a good impression on your co-workers and on the person you are talking to on the phone.

Conversation:

A: Hello. Geisert Corporation. Mark Edwards speaking.
B: Hello. This is Kevin James from North Horn Finance.

  May I speak to Tom Baker, please? (or)
  Could I please speak to Tom Baker?

A: I'm sorry. Tom Baker is not at his desk. (or)
  Mr. Baker is on vacation today.

A: Would you like to leave a message? (or)
  Can I take a message? (or)
B: Can you take a message? (or)
  Can I leave a message?

A/B: Yes.
B: Could you ask him to call me back? My telephone number is _____.
A: I'm sorry, could I have your name again, please?
B: My name is Kevin James.
A: And who do you work for?
B: I work for North Horn Finance.
A: Let me make sure I understand. You want Mr. Baker to call you back. Your name is Kevin James, you work for North Horn Finance, and your phone number is _____. Is that correct?
B: Yes, that's correct. / No, that isn't correct.
A: I'll give him the message. Is there anything else I can do for you?
B: No, that's everything. Thank you for your help.
A: It's my pleasure.
B: Good-bye.
A: Good-bye.

PERFORMANCE 8.1 – STUDENT A

 Work with a partner. Write your partner's manager's name in the space below.

_____

 Use the data below to practice the conversation on page 56. Make ten phone calls. Call your partner and ask for your partner's manager. He or she isn't there, so leave a message (ask for the manager to call you back). Do not look at page 58.

YOU	YOUR COMPANY	YOUR PHONE
Bill Erickson	Erickson Electronics	798-968-2649
Bob Freshman	St. James Metal Company	991-487-2261
Joe Alexander	Wycoff Supply Company	792-741-2870
Julie Rampart	Nichols Packaging Company	691-684-7910
Sandy McCormick	Adduce Advertising	398-852-5319
Bernice Schaefer	Alsace Insurance	891-890-0927
Art Michaels	East Williams Air Transport	398-502-4351
Bill Malone	Blue Onion Sporting Goods	498-871-4051
Alex Swanson	Angina Decorating Incorporated	299-602-5417
Wilbert Manchaca	I C F Office Supplies	498-701-4864

PERFORMANCE 8.1 – STUDENT B

 Work with a partner. Write your partner's manager's name in the space below.

_____

 Use the data below to practice the conversation on page 56. Make ten phone calls. Call your partner and ask for your partner's manager. He or she isn't there, so leave a message (ask for the manager to call you back). Do not look at page 57.

YOU	YOUR COMPANY	YOUR PHONE
Joe Phillips	Maritime Marine	499-692-5603
Kyle Stephan	Southwest Auto Sales	399-677-7611
Sally Rogers	Nevada Paper Company	491-260-0279
Pete McDowell	Vineyard Galleries	796-479-7279
John Williams	Madison Guarantee Incorporated	394-987-7164
Matthew Edwards	Yellow Circle Books	690-581-2573
Richard McGill	Wooden Dove Catering	396-975-4965
Polly Beavis	West Reynaldo Motors	594-875-9712
Butch Gilbert	Blue Missouri Mortgage Company	394-788-4545
Hector Garcia	Spanish Bluffs Apartments	996-431-8891

PERFORMANCE 8.2 – STUDENT A

 Work with a partner. Write your partner's manager's name in the space below.

_____

 Use the data below to practice the conversation on page 56. Make six phone calls. Call your partner and ask for your partner's manager. He or she isn't there, so leave a message (ask for the manager to call you back). Do not look at page 60.

Note:
(783) 342-9987 Ext. 329 =
area code seven eight three, three four two nine nine eight seven, extension three two nine

YOU	YOUR COMPANY	YOUR PHONE
Bill Huffington	Purple Engine Magazine	(399) 486-8103
Tom Jackson	Southern Blue Apple Company	(392) 852-3592
Mike Preston	Lime Goods Marketing	(593) 321-6343
Tom Arnoldson	Jett Brook Electric	(793) 342-9987 Ext.329
Nancy Rubout	Baker Power Company	(396) 2324-6668
Barry Solbership	Blodgett Finance	(594) 523-7890

PERFORMANCE 8.2 – STUDENT B

Work with a partner. Write your partner's manager's name in the space below.

_____

Use the data below to practice the conversation on page 56. Make six phone calls. Call your partner and ask for your partner's manager. He or she isn't there, so leave a message (ask for the manager to call you back). Do not look at page 59.

Note:
(783) 342-9987 Ext. 329 =
area code seven eight three, three four two nine nine eight seven, extension three two nine

YOU	YOUR COMPANY	YOUR PHONE
Vince Rockenston	Belmont Island Travel	(594) 221-5401
Matthew Richardson	Fairview Meyers Investment Services	(699) 465-0450
Norm Crosby	East Ogden Systems	(897) 668-8208
Mary Wilson	Victor Benton Incorporated	(396) 787-9994 Ext. 332
Kevin Jametson	Blue Summit Paintings	(392) 554-1212
Mark Edwards	Randall Lyman Auto Parts	(896) 423-8974

PERFORMANCE 8.3 – STUDENT A

 Work with a partner. Practice taking and leaving telephone messages. Do not look at page 62.

1. You are Bruce Phillips. Your phone number is 296-747-3977. You work for Silver Donkey Airlines. Call Mr. Williams. If he is not there, have him call you back.

2. Mr. Birch will be in Italy until Friday. Take a message.

3. You are Hideaki Huffington. You work for Eastern Rainfall Company. Your phone number is 599-848-5225. Call Ms. Blueberry. If she is not there, have her call you back.

4. Mr. Scanzoni is on a business trip. He will be back Wednesday afternoon. Take a message.

5. You are Josh Pebbleton. You work for Big Black Pipe Company. Your telephone number is 494-893-5784. Call Mr. Tanaka. If he is not there, ask him to call you back.

6. Ms. Curtiss is in Saipan this week. She will be back next Monday. Take a message.

7. You are Gary Potter. You work for Happy Jack Advertising. Your telephone number is 892-045-5467. Call Mr. French. If he is not there, have him call you back.

8. Mr. Williamson is in Paris. He will be back on Friday. Take a message.

PERFORMANCE 8.4 – STUDENT A

 Work with a partner. Practice taking and leaving telephone messages.

1. You are Tom McHenry. You work for Lead Pipe Finance. Your telephone number is 295-743-7445. Call Ms. Honda. If she is not there, have her call you back.

2. Mr. Chen is in Hong Kong until tomorrow evening. Take a message.

3. Your name is Joe Jacobson. You work for Copper Avenue Mortgage. Call Mr. Farmer. If he is not there, have him call you back at 599-055-7557.

4. Mr. Yamamoto is sick today. However, he may be back in the office later this afternoon. Take a message.

5. You are Thomas Monroe. You work for Greenback Paints. Call Mr. Rogers. If he is not in, have him call you back at 797-540-7843.

6. Mr. Son is in Hawaii this week. He will be back next Tuesday. Take a message.

7. You are Ralph Cage. You work for Alpha Franklin Cosmetics. Call Ms. Davis. If she isn't there, have her call you back at 598-654-0861.

8. Ms. Dulling is on vacation in Mexico. She will be back on Monday. Take a message.

PERFORMANCE 8.3 – STUDENT B

 Work with a partner. Practice taking and leaving telephone messages. Do not look at page 61.

1. Mr. Williams is visiting a customer in London. He will be back in the office tomorrow morning. Take a message.

2. You are James Linden. You work for Pink Highland Rental Company. Your telephone number is 794-838-2055. Call Mr. Birch. If he is not available, have him call you back.

3. Ms. Blueberry is visiting a supplier until 11 a.m. today. Take a message.

4. You are Karen Archacki. You work for Green Milk Unlimited. Your telephone number is 593-535-7662. Call Mr. Scanzoni. If he is not available, have him call you back.

5. Mr. Tanaka is attending his daughter's college graduation ceremony today. He will be back tomorrow. Take a message.

6. You are Beth Clark. You work for Black Sky Airlines. Call Ms. Curtiss. If she is unavailable, have her call you back at 996-920-0073.

7. Mr. French is in Scotland this week. He won't be back until next week. Take a message.

8. You are Mary Fujiwara. You work for Red Ink Publishing. Call Mr. Williamson. If he isn't there, have him call you back at 495-456-0540.

PERFORMANCE 8.4 – STUDENT B

 Work with a partner. Practice taking and leaving telephone messages.

1. Ms. Honda is visiting a customer in Argentina. She will be back on Tuesday afternoon. Take a message.

2. You are Ted James. You work for Green Hat Security. Your phone number is 794-454-4968. Please call Mr. Chen. If he is not available, have him call you back.

3. Mr. Farmer will be visiting a customer until 2 p.m. today. Take a message.

4. You are Dawn Hires. You work for Big White Shoe Incorporated. Call Mr. Yamamoto. If he is not available, have him call you back at 592-789-4021.

5. Mr. Rogers is meeting with his lawyer. He will be back tomorrow. Take a message.

6. You are Jennifer Van Houston. You work for South Coast Airlines. Call Mr. Son. If he is unavailable, have him call you back. Your telephone number is 996-364-7846.

7. Ms. Davis is in Thailand this week. She will return on Wednesday. Take a message.

8. You are Johnny Tenuta. You work for Heitz Hauling. Call Ms. Dulling. If she isn't there, have her call you back at 595-840-6540.

PERFORMANCE 8.5

Create a conversation. Rewrite each sentence, putting the words in the correct order, or respond appropriately.

A: _____
(Black Box is Bill hello speaking Airlines this Jackson)

B: _____
(John please Smith hello this is speak Susan from to DEKL Company may Williams I)

A: _____ .

_____ ?
(I'm take sorry a Mr. isn't right here now can Williams message I)

B: _____

_____
(you yes ask to is call telephone me back could 791-154-5616 my him number)

A: _____
(I name please again have could your)

B: _____

A: _____

B: _____
(spelled Smith S-m-i-t-h is)

A: _____

B: I work for DEKL Company.

A: _____
You said your name is Susan Smith, you work for DEKL Company and your telephone number
is 791-154-5616. _____ ?

B: _____

A: _____ .

_____ ?

B: No, that's everything.

A: _____ .

A: It's my pleasure.
B: Good-bye.
A: Good-bye.

PERFORMANCE 8.6 - STUDENT A – PART 1

You work for Green Ice Cooling Systems. A newspaper reporter is going to call you on the telephone. Here is some information about your company.

- Established: 1965
- Main Products: air conditioners
- Main Customers: large hotels
- Head Office: Phoenix, Arizona, USA
- Factories: Colorado and Arizona
- Employees: 2,400 total (400 in the head office and 1,000 in each factory)
- Sales in 1999: $573,842,837

PERFORMANCE 8.6 - STUDENT A – PART 2

You are a magazine reporter. You have been assigned to write a story about Edward Tires. Call and find out the following information:

Established: _____

Main Products: _____

Main Customers: _____

Head Office: _____

Factories: _____

Employees: _____

Sales in 2001: _____

PERFORMANCE 8.6 -STUDENT B – PART 1

You are a newspaper reporter. You are writing a story about Green Ice Cooling Systems. Call and find out the following information:

Established: _____

Main Products: _____

Main Customers: _____

Head Office: _____

Factories: _____

Employees: _____

Annual Sales in 1999: _____

PERFORMANCE 8.6 -STUDENT B – PART 2

You work for Edward Tires. A reporter will call you. Here is some information about your company.

- Established: 1945
- Main Products: aircraft tires
- Main Customer: Boeing
- Head Office: Fresno, California
- Factories: Wisconsin, Ohio and California
- Employees: 6,300 total (300 in the head office and 2,000 in each factory)
- Sales in 2001: $453,835,417,292

PERFORMANCE 8.7 - STUDENT A

Work with a partner. Practice taking and leaving telephone messages.

1. Call Linscott Grant Corporation and ask for Mr. Edwards. If he isn't there, leave your name and number.

2. You work for Purple Pencil Company. Your supervisor, Ms. Vanderbilt, is buying office furniture today and won't be back until 5 p.m.

3. You are a reporter. Call and ask about the following questions about the company where Student B works.

   Company: _____

   Company President: _____

   Established: _____

   Main Products: _____

   Main Customer: _____

   Head Office: _____

   Factories: _____

   Employees: _____

   Annual Sales: _____

4. A reporter is going to call you. Answer questions about the company where you work.

PERFORMANCE 8.7 – STUDENT B

Work with a partner. Practice taking and leaving telephone messages.

1. You work for Linscott Grant Corporation. Your boss, Mr. Edwards, will be in Africa on a business trip until next week.

2. Call Purple Pencil Company and ask for Ms. Vanderbilt. If she isn't there, ask her to call you back.

3. A reporter is going to call you. Answer questions about the company where you work.

4. You are a reporter. Call and ask these questions about the company where Student A works.

Company: _____

Company President: _____

Established: _____

Employees: _____

Main Products: _____

Head Office: _____

Factories: _____

Main Customer: _____

Annual Sales: _____

Skill 8:
Take or leave a telephone message

EVALUATION

When the phone rings at work, I can immediately speak English.

I have memorized the phrases for taking a message on the telephone.

I have memorized the phrases for leaving a message on the telephone.

I can take a message without using eye contact or gestures.

I can take a message from a native English speaker on the telephone in real life.

Three months from now, I will still remember the phrases needed for taking or leaving a message on the telephone.

Skill 9: Change topics

Skill 9:
Change topics

 GOALS:
Politely change the topic of a conversation.

BENEFITS:
You can get other people to talk about something interesting. You can avoid talking about things that you are not interested in.

 **Phrases:**

By the way... (new topic)

I hate to change the subject, but...(new topic)

Speaking of.... (to change to a related topic)

Anyway...
(to return to a topic you already talked about)

Examples:

By the way, has anyone here ever visited the branch office in Madrid?

I hate to change the subject, but has anyone here visited the branch office in Madrid?

Speaking of Spain, has anyone here ever visited the branch office in Madrid?

Anyway, I am really excited about going to the branch office in Madrid.

PERFORMANCE 9.1

Your instructor will write a topic on the board. Start a conversation on the topic. After two minutes, the instructor will write a new topic on the board. Change to the new topic.

PERFORMANCE 9.2

Work in small groups. Make a list of six things you would like to talk about.

1. _____

2. _____

3. _____

4. _____

5. _____

6. _____

Now, take turns changing to new topics. Continue until you have discussed all of the topics.

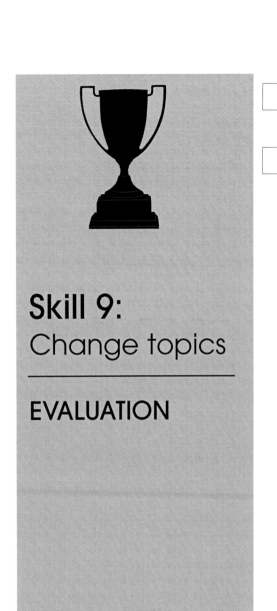

Skill 9:
Change topics

EVALUATION

☐ I have memorized the phrases for changing topics.

☐ If I am talking with a native English speaker in real life, I will have the confidence to change topics if I am not interested in the discussion.

Skill 10: Ask for or give advice

Skill 10:
Ask for or give advice

 GOALS:
Be able to ask for or give advice to a native English speaker.

 BENEFITS:
You can learn things from other people. You can improve your life with other people's recommendations. You can help other people by giving them suggestions.

What do you think I should....?
Where do you think I should...?
How do you think I should...?
Which _____ do you think I should...?

I think you should... (verb: go to the hospital)
I recommend... (noun: pizza, going to the hospital)

Notes:
When you feel strongly about your advice, use the word "definitely," like this:
I definitely think you should...
(verb: go to the hospital)

When you don't feel strong about your advice, use the word "consider," like this:
I think you should consider...
(noun: going to the hospital)

What do you think I should buy?
Where do you think I should go?
How do you think I should tell Mr. Smith that I forgot to mail the proposal?
Which copier do you think we should buy?

PERFORMANCE 10.1

 Work with a partner. Take turns asking for and giving advice about the following topics.

- what to give your customer for Christmas
- what to give your boss for her birthday
- where to go for your next vacation
- which new computer to buy
- where to hold the sales meeting
- where to buy a new car
- where to rent telephone equipment
- which digital camera to buy
- where to take your client to lunch

PERFORMANCE 10.2

Write down 10 problems you have. Next, tell your problems to another classmate and ask for advice. When you are finished, change partners, and ask for advice from a different classmate. Did both classmates give you the same advice?

1. _____

2. _____

3. _____

4. _____

5. _____

6. _____

7. _____

8. _____

9. _____

10. _____

PERFORMANCE 10.3

John Livingston is a management trainee from a different country coming to your company for three months. He is single and 22 years old. He doesn't know very much about your country. Write an e-mail to Mr. Livingston, giving him some advice about living in your country and working for your company.

_____

_____

_____

_____

_____

_____

_____

_____

_____

_____

_____

_____

_____

_____

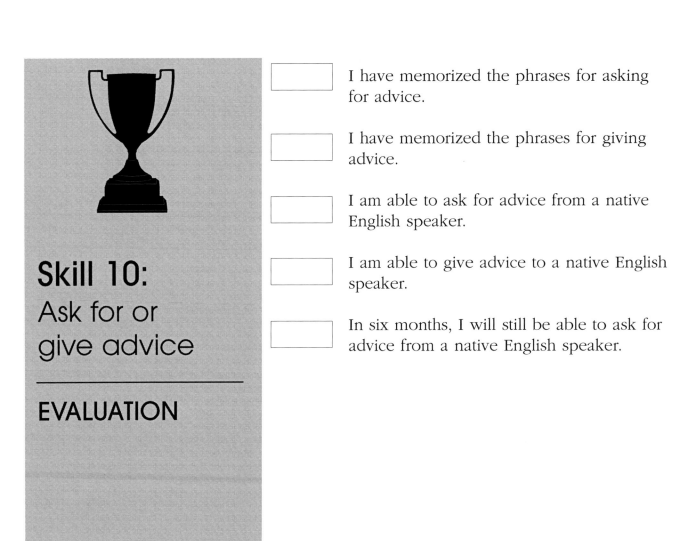

Skill 10:
Ask for or give advice

EVALUATION

☐ I have memorized the phrases for asking for advice.

☐ I have memorized the phrases for giving advice.

☐ I am able to ask for advice from a native English speaker.

☐ I am able to give advice to a native English speaker.

☐ In six months, I will still be able to ask for advice from a native English speaker.

Skill 11: Make, accept or decline an invitation

Skill 11:
Make, accept or decline an invitation

 GOALS:
Invite a native English speaker to lunch or dinner. Accept an invitation from a native English speaker. Politely decline an invitation and give a reason. Speak loudly and clearly. Be confident and energetic when making an invitation. Confirm the meeting time and place.

BENEFITS:
You will be able to eat, drink, and have fun with native English speakers.

 **Conversation:**

(making an invitation, accepting an invitation):

A: Do you like hamburgers?

B: Yes.

A: Great, let's go to McDonald's together. (or)

Great, let's ____ together.

B: OK.

A: What day shall we go?

B: Let's go on Friday.

A: Where shall we meet?

B: Let's meet at the Tokyo Station, in front of McDonald's.

A: What time shall we meet?

B: Let's meet at 5 p.m.

A: Let me make sure I understand. I'll meet you at the Tokyo Station, in front of McDonald's at 5 p.m. on Friday. Is that correct?

B: Yes, that's correct.

A: OK, see you then.

B: See you then.

PERFORMANCE 11.1

Work with a partner. Take turns making and accepting invitations about the following topics.

- eat pizza
- play cards
- have a drink after work
- go to Starbucks for coffee
- go see a movie
- play golf

- go sightseeing on Sunday
- go dancing
- sing karaoke
- go to the beach
- go out to dinner
- go to an amusement park

Phrases (declining an invitation):
When you decline an invitation, suggest a different time.

> I'm afraid I'm busy that day.
> I'm sorry. I already have something planned on Monday night.

> How about next Saturday?
> How about next Friday afternoon instead?

Conversation:

> A: What day shall we go?
> B: How about Thursday?
> A: I'm afraid I'm busy on Thursday. How about Friday?
> B: I'm sorry. I already have something planned on Friday.

If you cannot agree on a time to meet with the other person, use this expression:

> A: Well, let's get together sometime.
> B: Yes, let's do that.

PERFORMANCE 11.2

A: Make invitations for the following situations.
B: Decline the invitation and suggest another time.

- go camping this weekend
- go swimming
- play ping-pong
- go to a concert
- play video games
- go to a baseball game

- play basketball
- go to the horse races
- go parasailing
- go shopping
- go scuba diving

PERFORMANCE 11.3

Practice making appointments with other students in your class. Use the calendar below to help you.

	Sunday	Monday	Tuesday	Wednesday	Thursday	Friday	Saturday
8:00 a.m.							
9:00 a.m.							
10:00 a.m.							
11:00 a.m.							
12:00 p.m.							
1:00 p.m.							
2:00 p.m.							
3:00 p.m.							
4:00 p.m.							
5:00 p.m.							

Skill 11:
Make, accept or decline an invitation

EVALUATION

☐ I have memorized the phrases for making and accepting invitations.

☐ I will remember how to use "Well, let's get together sometime."

☐ I am energetic and enthusiastic when I make an invitation.

☐ I am confident in my ability to ask a native English speaker to lunch or dinner.

☐ I can easily confirm the meeting time and place so there will be no miscommunication.

☐ I am able to politely decline an invitation.

☐ One year from now, I will still remember the phrases needed for making, accepting and declining an invitation.

Skill 12: Offer help

Skill 12:
Offer help

Phrases:

GOALS:
Offer to help someone. Accept or decline help when someone asks to help you. Speak clearly and loudly. Be energetic when offering help.

BENEFITS:
You will be able to help a native English speaker when he or she needs help. If a native English speaker wants to help you, you will know what to say to accept or decline the offer.

A: (says problem)

B: Do you want me to…. (or)
Do you want me to do it? (or)
Do you want me to call him? (or)
Do you want me to help you with your luggage? (or)
Do you want me to help you get there?

A: Yes, thank you. (or)
No, that's OK. Thank you anyway.

If someone refuses an offer, ask a second time to be polite. Look at the example.

A: I'm having problems with the fax machine.

B: Do you want me to help you use the fax machine?

A: No, that's OK. Thank you anyway.

B: Are you sure?

A: Yes. That's OK. (or)
Well, OK. Thank you.

PERFORMANCE 12.1

Work with a partner. Take turns making offers. Use the sentences below.

- My computer is broken.
- I don't know how to get to New York from here.
- I don't know where to find the nearest drugstore.
- I forgot how to use the copier.
- I don't know where to catch the train for the airport.
- I don't know how to get downtown.
- I don't have enough time to finish my report.
- I have a sore throat.
- I lost my computer on the train.
- I need to have an eye exam, but I can't speak the language here.
- I'm nervous about making a presentation in English.
- I don't understand the minutes from yesterday's meeting.
- I'm hungry, but I don't have time to go to McDonald's.
- I'm not going to finish this report before the deadline.

PERFORMANCE 12.2

Go back to Performance 10.2. Tell your partner your problem, but don't ask for advice. This time your partner will offer to help you. Accept or politely decline the offer.

Skill 12:
Offer help

EVALUATION

☐ I have memorized the phrases for offering to help someone.

☐ I can make my own phrases for offering to help someone based on the examples.

☐ If I see a native English speaker who seems to need help, I will be able to offer help, because I have confidence in my ability.

☐ I have memorized the phrases for accepting or declining help.

☐ If I don't want a native English speaker to help me, I can use the phrases to politely decline the offer.

☐ After studying this lesson, I am more likely to offer help to a native English speaker.

Skill 13: Make a request

Skill 13:
Make a request

GOALS:
Ask for things you need. Politely decline requests from other people. Give a good reason for declining the request. Politely agree to requests.

BENEFITS:
You can get other people to give you things you need. You can get other people to help you. You can stop native English speakers from making you do things you don't want to do.

Phrases: (making a request)

Could you please...

Could I please...

Could you please make 10 copies of this document?

Could I please go home early today?

Phrases: (agreeing)

Sure.

OK.

No problem.

Phrases: (declining)

Give a good reason why you can't help when you decline a request.

I'd like to say yes, but... (I'm using it right now).
I'd like to help you, but...

PERFORMANCE 13.1

A: Ask to use the following things.
B: Agree to all the requests. (without looking at the book, if possible)

- borrow – scissors
- lend – pen
- borrow – calculator
- lend – 10 dollars
- borrow – dictionary
- lend – eraser

- borrow – ruler
- lend – CD player
- borrow – glue
- lend – laptop computer
- borrow – stapler
- lend – pencil

Now, Student B, ask for each item to be returned. Use the phrase
"Could you please return my ——— ?" or " Could I please have my ——— back?"

PERFORMANCE 13.2

A: Make requests.
B: Decline all the requests (without looking at the book, if possible).

- borrow – newspaper
- lend – 500 dollars
- do my homework for me
- help me move into my new apartment tomorrow
- a cigarette

- a dictionary
- put more paper into the printer
- buy – a pitcher of beer
- lend – laptop computer
- borrow – your car
- lend – truck

Conversation (confirming):

A: Could you please lend me five dollars?
B: Let me make sure I understand. You want me to lend you five dollars. Is that correct?
A: Yes, that's correct.
B: Sure. (or) I'd like to help you but….

PERFORMANCE 13.3

A: Make requests
B: Confirm all requests, then either accept or decline the request
(without looking at the book, if possible).

- borrow – laptop computer battery
- lend – yellow highlighter
- Erase the board.
- Turn off the lights.
- Close the door.
- Give me your expense report.

- Rewrite the minutes from last Thursday's meeting.
- Clear the paper jam in the copier.
- Go to the store and buy a replacement ink cartridge for the printer.

PERFORMANCE 13.4

Make a list of 20 things that you use to do your job. Next, ask your classmates for them. Your classmates should confirm the request and either accept or decline the request.

1. _____

2. _____

3. _____

4. _____

5. _____

6. _____

7. _____

8. _____

9. _____

10. _____

11. _____

12. _____

13. _____

14. _____

15. _____

16. _____

17. _____

18. _____

19. _____

20. _____

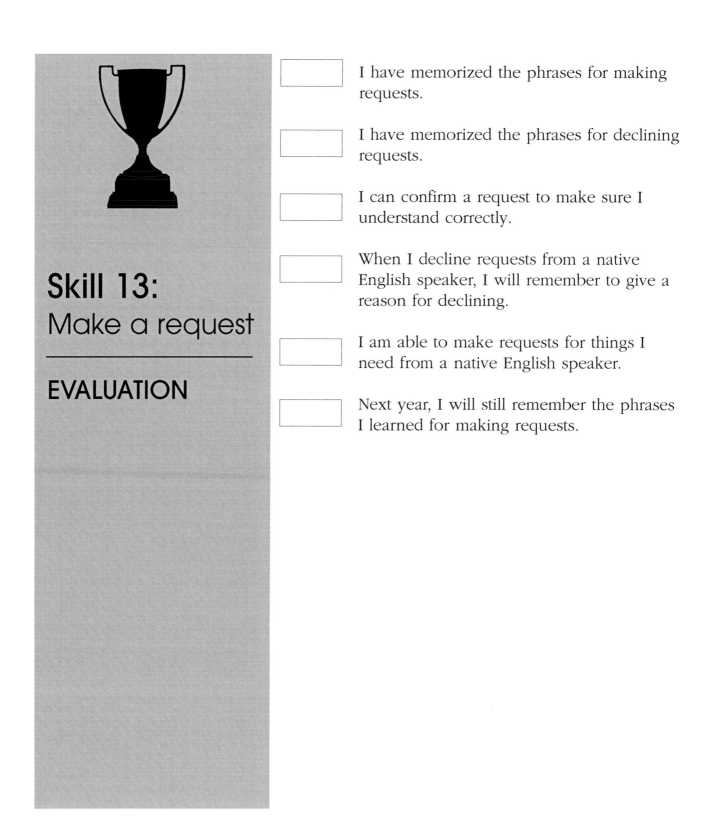

Skill 13:
Make a request

EVALUATION

☐ I have memorized the phrases for making requests.

☐ I have memorized the phrases for declining requests.

☐ I can confirm a request to make sure I understand correctly.

☐ When I decline requests from a native English speaker, I will remember to give a reason for declining.

☐ I am able to make requests for things I need from a native English speaker.

☐ Next year, I will still remember the phrases I learned for making requests.

Skill 14: Apologize

Skill 14:
Apologize

 **GOALS:**
Apologize when you make a mistake. Offer to help fix the problem you created. Politely accept apologies from other people.

BENEFITS:
When you make mistakes, you will be able to minimize the problem by apologizing. You will be able to offer help. Your customers and co-workers will appreciate your honesty and your willingness to correct the mistake.

 **Phrases:**

A: I want to apologize. I'm very sorry that…(bad thing that happened)

A : I'll… (way to help fix the problem)
I'll be happy to replace it. (or)
I'll buy you a new one. (or)
I'll make sure it doesn't happen again.

B: Well, it's OK this time, but let's try to make sure it doesn't happen again. (or)
Don't worry about it. (or)
That's OK. It's no problem.
OK. Thank you.

Conversation:

A: I want to apologize. I'm very sorry that I was 10 minutes late for work. I'll stay overtime this evening to finish all my work.

B: Well, it's OK this time, but let's try to make sure it doesn't happen again.

PERFORMANCE 14.1

Work with a partner. Take turns asking for and accepting apologies for the situations below.

- You spilled coffee on your partner's computer keyboard.
- You dropped your partner's laptop computer.
- You forgot to turn in your expense report on time.
- You sent your partner the wrong invoice.
- You shipped broken products to your partner.
- You forgot to go to a meeting with your partner.
- You were late for your English language training class.
- You lost the purchase order that your partner sent you.
- You lost your temper and yelled at your partner yesterday.
- You forgot to return the $100 that you borrowed from your partner last week.

PERFORMANCE 14.2

Now make your own situations and practice with a classmate.

1. _____

2. _____

3. _____

4. _____

5. _____

6. _____

7. _____

8. _____

9. _____

10. _____

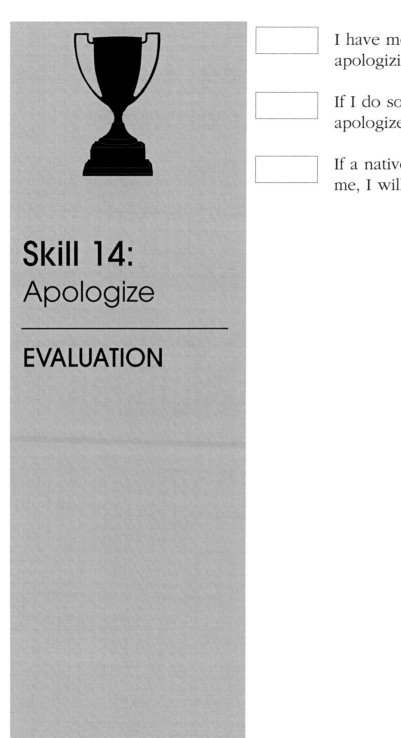

Skill 14:
Apologize

EVALUATION

☐ I have memorized the phrases for apologizing.

☐ If I do something wrong, I will be able to apologize to a native English speaker.

☐ If a native English speaker apologizes to me, I will know what to say.

Skill 15: Show sympathy

Skill 15:
Show sympathy

GOALS:
Be able to show sympathy to a native English speaker when something bad happens. Respond appropriately when someone shows sympathy to you.

BENEFITS:
You will make the other person feel better if you show sympathy. It would be rude if, for example, you were the only person who didn't show sympathy to a co-worker whose husband had died. During times of tragedy, it is especially important to be able to use certain polite, appropriate phrases.

Phrases:

A: That's too bad.

   I'm sorry to hear that. (heard directly)

   I was sorry to hear about…

   (heard through a different person)

B: Thank you.

   Thank you very much. I appreciate your concern.

PERFORMANCE 15.1

Work with a partner. Take turns expressing and accepting sympathy for the situations below.

A: What's wrong?
B: (Say the problem below.)
A: (Show sympathy.)

- You did badly on a TOEIC test.
- You lost your passport.
- Your grandfather passed away.
- You accidentally deleted an important computer file.
- You didn't get a promotion you thought you deserved.
- You have a terrible cold.
- Your dog died.
- You got a bad performance review.
- Your customer decided to no longer use your services.
- Your boss got angry.
- You didn't make the sales goal.
- You accidentally threw away a sales contract.

PERFORMANCE 15.2

Show sympathy to your classmate about things you heard from someone else.

1. You heard from Mr. Smith that your classmate's grandmother died.
2. You heard from Mr. Jones that your classmate's husband/wife was in the hospital.
3. You heard from Mr. Smith that your classmate's daughter was injured in a traffic accident.
4. You heard from Mr. Jones that your classmate's father lost his job.
5. You heard from Mr. Smith that your classmate's wife broke her leg.

PERFORMANCE 15.3

Make your own situations as in Performance 15.2 and practice with a classmate.

1. _____

2. _____

3. _____

4. _____

5. _____

6. _____

7. _____

PERFORMANCE 15.4

Combine showing sympathy with making an offer. Look at the conversation.

A: What's wrong?
B: I lost my wallet.
A: Oh, I'm sorry to hear that.
B: Thank you. I appreciate your concern.
A: Do you want me to loan you some money?
B: That's OK. Thank you anyway.
A: Are you sure?
B: Yes, that's OK.

Work with a partner. Use these problems. Try to do the conversations without looking at the book.

- You can't find your car keys.
- You just threw up in the bathroom.
- Your computer crashed.
- Your boss asked you to send faxes to 100 customers.
- The copier got a paper jam.
- You spilled coffee all over yourself.
- Your car got a flat tire.

Skill 15:
Show sympathy

EVALUATION

☐ I have memorized the phrases showing sympathy.

☐ I understand the difference between "I'm sorry to hear that" and "I was sorry to hear about...."

☐ Even though I won't use the phrases very often, I practiced showing sympathy enough that I will still remember the phrases years from now.

☐ If something bad happens to a native English speaker, I will be able to show sympathy.

☐ If something bad happens to me, I will know what to say when a native English speaker shows me sympathy.

Skill 16: Ask for and give examples

Skill 16:
Ask for and give examples

 GOALS:
Speak quickly. Speak clearly. Ask for an example. Give a specific example.

BENEFITS:
Examples are often necessary to prove your point. If someone is talking and not providing examples, you will be able to ask for specific examples. Asking for examples is also a good way for you to improve your understanding.

Phrases:

Could you give me an example?
Could you give me a specific example?
Let me give you an example.

Conversation 1:

A: Mr. Tanaka sometimes forgets to do his homework.

B: Could you give me a specific example?

A: Yes. On March 7th, 2003, he did not do his homework.

Conversation 2:

A: Mr. Tanaka sometimes forgets to do his homework.

B: Oh, really?

A: Yes, let me give you an example. On March 7, 2003, he did not do his homework.

PERFORMANCE 16.1

Work with a partner. Take turns asking for and giving examples. Student A, start by reading the sentences below. Student B try to do the conversations without looking at the book.

- The United States has many interesting places to visit.

- I sometimes sleep in the afternoon.

- I sometimes eat at Chinese restaurants.

- I enjoy having dinner with my friends.

- I like watching some television programs.

- My company sells many quality products.

- I sometimes ride in a taxi.

- We have received some complaints about our new product.

- I occasionally eat too much.

- I like to play sports.

- I sometimes eat at McDonalds.

- Sometimes it rains very hard.

- Sometimes my boss is disappointed with me.

- I sometimes get angry with some of my coworkers.

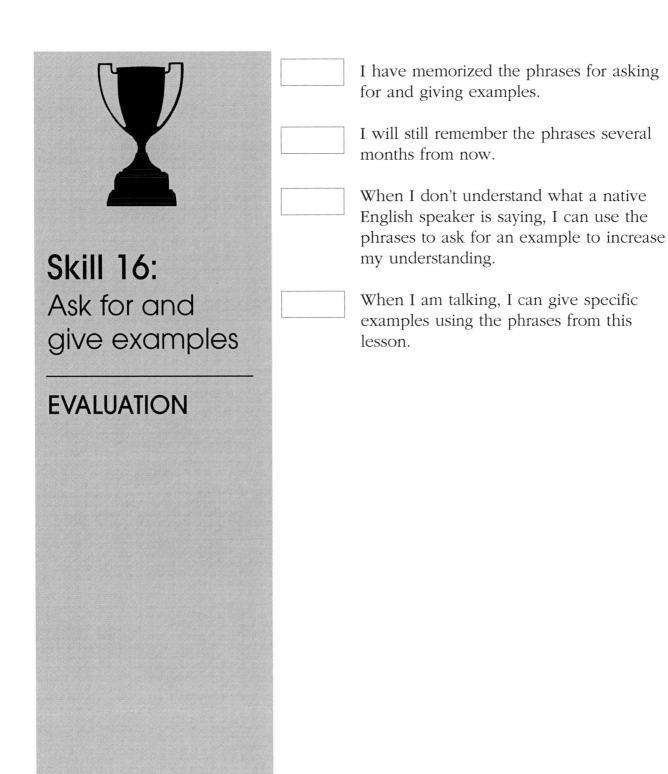

Skill 16:
Ask for and give examples

EVALUATION

☐ I have memorized the phrases for asking for and giving examples.

☐ I will still remember the phrases several months from now.

☐ When I don't understand what a native English speaker is saying, I can use the phrases to ask for an example to increase my understanding.

☐ When I am talking, I can give specific examples using the phrases from this lesson.

Skill 17: Hesitate

Skill 17:
Hesitate

GOALS:
Avoid silence.
Someone should be
making sounds at all times during
a conversation. Always make
some kind of sound when you
are thinking and don't know
what to say.

BENEFITS:
Silence often makes
native English
speakers uncomfortable. If
someone asks you a question,
and you need time to think about
an answer, you need to make
sounds. This will tell the other
person that you heard and
understood the question, but that
you need time to think about an
answer.

Phrases:

Uummmmmm, let me see.

Ahh, just a moment.

Gestures:

(Scratch your head.)

(Touch your chin.)

(Tilt your head.)

PERFORMANCE 17.1

Work with a partner. Take turns. Practice hesitating before answering each question.

Student A

- How old were you when you entered high school?
- What day of the week did you go on your first date?
- How long does it take to fly from Tokyo to London?
- What year did you learn to ride a bicycle?
- When was the last time you drank milk?
- What does "CIA" stand for?
- How much does it cost to fly from New York to Paris?
- What is the name of the last video that you rented?
- Close your eyes. What color are your teacher's eyes?

Student B

- What time did you get up last Saturday morning?
- How much coffee did you drink last week?
- Close your eyes. How many people in this room are wearing a necktie?
- What did you eat for dinner last Sunday night?
- What is the warmest place you have ever visited?
- What was your phone number when you were a child?
- When was the last time you ate at McDonald's?
- How many times have you taken a shower this month?
- What was your first grade teacher's name?

Skill 17:
Hesitate

EVALUATION

☐ I have memorized the phrases and gestures for hesitating.

☐ When I am talking with a native English speaker, I avoid silence.

☐ I understand that it may make native English speakers uncomfortable for there to be long periods of silence during a conversation.

☐ I will remember to use both phrases and gestures when I need time to think.

Skill 18: Ask for, give and support an opinion

Skill 18:
Ask for, give and support an opinion

GOALS:
Ask someone which of two things they prefer and why. Check to make sure that you understood their opinion correctly. Give your opinion. Speak clearly and loudly. Give a clear reason to support your opinion.

BENEFITS:
You will be able to explain your opinion to a native English speaker. By giving a reason to support your opinion, you are more likely to convince the other person that your opinion is correct. If you are not sure you understand, you will be able to check for clarification.

Phrases:

A: Which do you think is better: ____ or ____?

B: I think ___ is better than ____ because _____.

A: Let me make sure I understand. You think ____ is better than _____ because _____. Is that correct?

B: Yes, that's correct. (or) No, that isn't correct. I think…..

PERFORMANCE 18.1

Work with a partner. Take turns practicing the conversation above using the words below. Make up your own reasons for preferring things. Try to do the conversations without looking at the book.

- KFC / McDonald's
- winter / summer
- soccer / American football
- playing golf / playing tennis
- working for a female manager / working for a male manager
- doing it now / waiting until later
- opening a sales office now / waiting until later to open a sales office
- hiring Mr. Phillips / hiring Mr. Jones
- going to London / going to Paris
- taking a boat to New York / flying to New York
- flying on American Airlines / flying on Singapore Airlines
- giving everyone a copy of the memo / emailing the memo to everyone
- launching a new product / spending money to advertise our old product
- making the product out of plastic / making the product out of metal
- studying English / studying accounting
- faxing the client our proposal / mailing the client our proposal
- having our customers fax us their orders / taking customer orders on the internet
- hiring two part time employees / hiring one full time employee
- borrowing money from a bank / selling stock to raise capital
- relocating our head office to a rural area / keeping the head office where it is now
- making the entire building non-smoking / allowing smoking in the break room only
- promoting employees based on their age / promoting employees based on their contributions
- asking women to resign after they get married / allowing women to continue working after marriage

PERFORMANCE 18.2

Make a list of related options like the ones in Performance 18.1 and ask a classmate which he or she prefers.

1._____

2._____

3._____

4._____

5._____

6._____

7._____

8._____

9._____

10._____

PERFORMANCE 18.3

Combine hesitating with asking for and giving an opinion. Look at the conversation.

A: Which do you think is better: ____ or ____?

B: Ummmmm, let me seeeeee. Ummm, I think ___ is better than ____ because _____.

A: Let me make sure I understand. You think ____ is better than _____ because _____. Is that correct?

B: Yes, that's correct. (or) No, that isn't correct. I think…..

Work with a partner. Try to do the conversations without looking at the book.

- orange juice / apple juice
- renting office space / building a new office
- putting advertisements into the newspaper / putting advertisements on television
- changing the color of our packaging / keeping our packaging the same color
- opening a new office in New York / opening a new office in London
- reducing employee salaries / reducing employee benefits
- hiring a new accountant / hiring a new office manager
- raising our dividend / repurchasing our company's stock

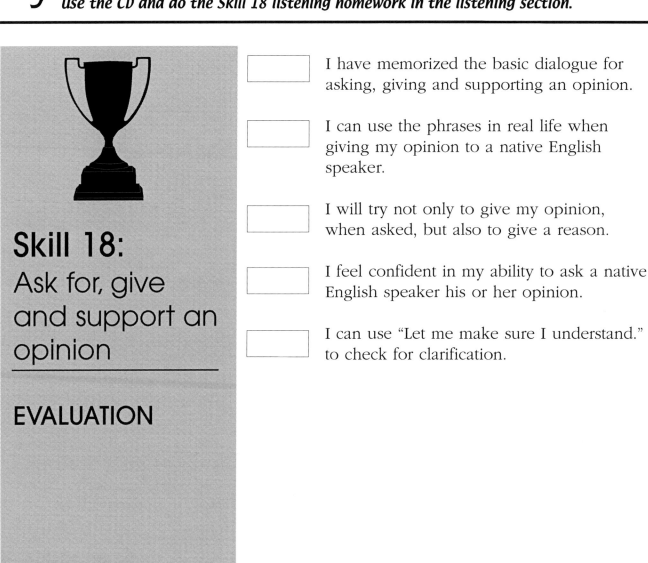

Skill 18:
Ask for, give and support an opinion

EVALUATION

☐ I have memorized the basic dialogue for asking, giving and supporting an opinion.

☐ I can use the phrases in real life when giving my opinion to a native English speaker.

☐ I will try not only to give my opinion, when asked, but also to give a reason.

☐ I feel confident in my ability to ask a native English speaker his or her opinion.

☐ I can use "Let me make sure I understand." to check for clarification.

Skill 19: Rephrase a question or an opinion

Skill 19:
Rephrase a question or an opinion

 GOALS:
Rephrase a question. Speak loudly and clearly. Rephrase someone's opinion.

BENEFITS:
You will be able to answer questions better if you understand the questions clearly. Rephrasing a question is also a way to give you more time to think of an answer. When rephrasing an opinion, you will be able to summarize what the other person has said. This will show the other person that you are listening and that you understand what the other person said. Also, sometimes people talk about the same thing for too long. Rephrasing an opinion is a good way to get the other person to move on to a new topic.

Phrases:

Let me make sure I understand. You want to know.... Is that correct?

Excuse me. Let me make sure I understand. You're saying.... Is that correct?

Conversation:
(question)

A: Did sales improve this quarter?
B: Let me make sure I understand. You want to know if sales improved this quarter. Is that correct?
A: Yes, that's correct.

Conversation:
(opinion)

A: I don't want to go scuba diving. It costs over $50 to rent equipment. To get to a good diving area, the boat crew charges $20. Food to feed the fish costs $15. In addition to that...

B: Excuse me. Let me make sure I understand. You are saying you don't want to go scuba diving because it costs too much. Is that correct?

PERFORMANCE 19.1

Your teacher will ask each of you some questions. Rephrase the questions.

PERFORMANCE 19.2

Work with a partner. Take turns asking questions and rephrasing them.

- What day of the week is it?
- Where is the bathroom?
- Did you use the fax machine yesterday?
- Why did Ms. Jones work until 11 p.m. last night?
- What time will you leave the office tonight?
- Where will your company manufacture your new product?
- How long have you been working for your company?
- Has Mr. Smith been the president of the company for a long time?

- What time is it right now in Madrid?
- What is Mr. Jones talking about?
- Why did you go to Tokyo last weekend?
- Did you get the email I sent you?
- Where are you going to hold the sales meeting?
- What time does your flight leave?
- Has your company been manufacturing plastic products since 1974?
- How long have you been studying English?

PERFORMANCE 19.3

*Combine hesitating, giving and supporting an opinion and rephrasing a question.
Look at the conversation.*

A: Which do you think is better: ___ or ____.
B: Let me make sure I understand. You want to know which I think is better: ____ or ___.
  Is that correct?
A: Yes, that's correct.
B: Ummmmmm, let me see. Ummmm. I think ____ is better than ___ because____.
A: Let me make sure I understand. You think ____ is better than ____ because ____. Is
  that correct?
B: Yes, that's correct. (or) No, that isn't correct.

Work with a partner. Try to do the conversations without looking at the book.

- going to the sales meeting / going to the production meeting
- buying a new copier / buying a new fax machine
- sending our customer an email / calling our customer on the phone
- shipping our products by airmail / shipping our products by regular mail
- designing a new product / improving our old product
- buying office equipment / renting office equipment
- giving Mr. Smith more training / firing Mr. Smith
- reducing our prices / using cheaper materials in our products

PERFORMANCE 19.4

 Your teacher will talk for too long about something. Interrupt your teacher and use the phrase "Excuse me. Let me make sure I understand. You're saying.... Is that correct?" to summarize his or her opinion.

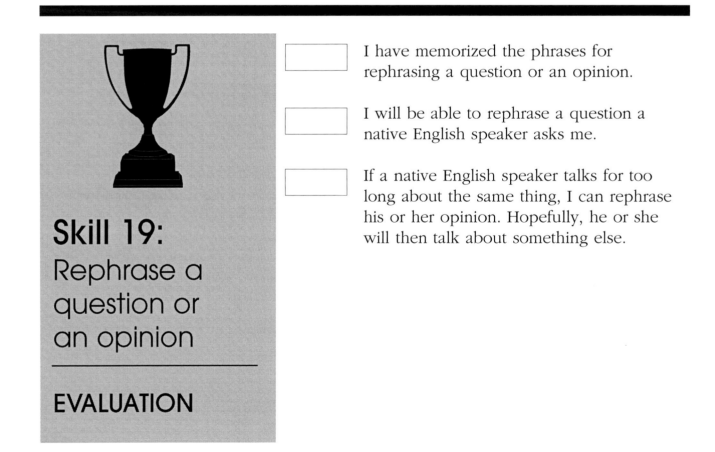

Skill 19:
Rephrase a
question or
an opinion

EVALUATION

I have memorized the phrases for rephrasing a question or an opinion.

I will be able to rephrase a question a native English speaker asks me.

If a native English speaker talks for too long about the same thing, I can rephrase his or her opinion. Hopefully, he or she will then talk about something else.

Skill 20: Make a toast

Skill 20:
Make a toast

 GOALS:
At a party, stand up, get everyone's attention and give a toast for a customer or co-worker. Speak very loudly so everyone can hear you clearly. Memorize the basic pattern for giving a toast. Practice the pattern so many times that even if you go to a party and have a little too much to drink, you will be able to remember the pattern and make a good toast in English.

BENEFITS:
You will be able to express your appreciation or happiness in front of a group of native English speakers.

 **Phrases:**

Could I have your attention?

We are all very happy today because …..

I want to thank _____ for _____, and also
I want to thank _____ for _____.

And finally, I propose a toast. To......

Cheers.

Example:

"Could I have your attention? We are all very happy today because we reached the sales goal. I want to thank Mr. Tanaka for being a very strict sales manager, and also, I want to thank Ms. Sasada for all her hard work in the administration department. I also want to thank all the sales people for all their hard work. Finally, I want to propose a toast. (Raise your glass and wait for everyone else to raise their glasses.) To all the hard work this year, and to making the sales goal again next year. Cheers." (applause)

The phrase 'To _____' is difficult. Talk about some good thing that you hope will happen in the future, or talk about the main person you are giving the toast for. Here are some examples:

- To success in your new job. (job promotion)
- To improving your TOEIC score.
- To Mr. and Mrs. James Burke. May you have a lifetime of happiness together. (wedding)

PERFORMANCE 20.1

Write a toast for something good that has happened. Here are some examples:

- A new employee has joined the staff.
- A staff member is going to get married.
- Someone was promoted to manager.
- Someone had a baby.

When you are done, your teacher will check what you have written. Next, practice the speech by yourself. When you are ready, give the toast to the entire class.

PERFORMANCE 20.2

Your teacher will give you a topic. You will have four minutes to create a toast and practice it. After the four minutes, give the toast to the class.

Skill 20:
Make a toast

EVALUATION

☐ I have memorized the basic pattern for giving a toast.

☐ In real life, if my boss asks me to give a toast at a party, I will be able to make a toast in English, using the phrases I memorized.

☐ I am able to make a toast in front of a large group of native English speakers.

Skill 21: Ask for a discount

Skill 21:
Ask for a discount

GOALS:
Politely ask for a discount for something that you want to buy. Give a good reason to support your request.

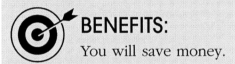

BENEFITS:
You will save money.

Phrases:

(reason for discount):

The product is damaged.

This product is very old.

I am interested in buying a large quantity.

I have done business with you for a long time.

(request for discount):

Perhaps you could give me a _____ percent discount.

Can you give me a _____ dollar discount?

Please give me a discount.

I cannot buy this product without a _____ yen discount.

Notes:

Use one sentence from the top group (reason), followed by one sentence from the bottom group (request). Here is an example:

"This product has a small scratch on it. Perhaps you could give me a 10% discount."

PERFORMANCE 21.1

Work with a partner. Take turns being a salesperson and a customer. Ask for a discount for the following items.

- Color TV – $1,200
- MP3 player – $100
- CD – $30
- Mobile Telephone – $70
- Used Car – $8,000

- Bicycle – $100
- Used Computer – $400
- Copier – $1,200
- DVD Player – $100
- Fax Machine – $80

I can save money in real life because I am able to ask for a discount.

I have memorized the basic phrases for asking for a discount.

Skill 21:
Ask for a discount

EVALUATION

Skill 22: Complain

Skill 22:
Complain

GOALS:
Explain why you are not satisfied with a product or service. Clearly explain what you need to be satisfied. Be strong and forceful, but not angry.

BENEFITS:
The service you receive will improve if you can clearly explain why you are not satisfied, and what specifically you want.

Phrases:

A: I hate to complain but.... (or)
I don't mean to complain, but... (or)
There is an issue we need to talk about.

My understanding was that____ was/were supposed to ____.
However, ... (problem)
Could you please ____.

B: (apologize – Skill 14)

Conversation 1:

A: There is an issue we need to talk about. My understanding was that the products we ordered were supposed to be made out of metal. However, the products you sold us are made out of plastic. Could you please send us new products made out of metal?

B: I want to apologize. I'm very sorry that we sent you the wrong products. I'll be happy to send you products made out of metal.

Conversation 2:

A: I hate to complain, but our understanding was that Mr. Jones was supposed to teach English from 7 o'clock to 9 o'clock. However, last Tuesday, he finished class at 8 o'clock. Could you please ask him to teach an additional hour next Tuesday?

B: I want to apologize. I'm very sorry that Mr. Jones misunderstood the schedule. I'll ask him to teach an additional hour next Tuesday.

PERFORMANCE 22.1

Work with a partner. Take turns complaining using the phrases below.

Product or Service	Your Understanding	Problem
rental car	4 doors	2 doors
product	made out of gold	silver
hotel room	king size bed	single bed
order	delivered on Monday	on Wednesday
product	12 inches long	10 inches long
flight	non-stop	layover in Chicago
rental car	red	white
operation manual	English	French
hotel room	ocean view	city view
table	non-smoking section	smoking section
computer monitor	color	monochrome
airplane seat	window	aisle
steak	well done	rare

When the problem is obvious, you do not need to say "my understanding was that..."

Conversation 1:

A: I don't mean to complain, but this soup is cold. Could you please bring me a bowl of hot soup?
B: I want to apologize. I'm sorry your soup is cold. I'll bring you another bowl right away.

Conversation 2:

A: I hate to complain, but the heater in our room is broken. Could you please fix it?
B: I want to apologize. I'm sorry your heater is broken. I'll send someone to your room right away to fix it.

PERFORMANCE 22.2

Work with a partner. Take turns complaining about the situations below.

- You never got the shipment of car parts you ordered.
- Your hotel room is too noisy.
- The windshield wipers on your rental car are broken.
- The computer monitor you bought is broken.
- The mobile phone you bought has no battery.
- Room service took two hours to bring you your lunch.
- The airline lost your suitcase.
- It's too cold in the room.

PERFORMANCE 22.3

Think of some problems that you want to complain about. Then practice with a classmate. Use both the long and shorter versions from 22.1 and 22.2.

1. _____

2. _____

3. _____

4. _____

5. _____

6. _____

7. _____

8. _____

9. _____

10. _____

Skill 22:
Complain

EVALUATION

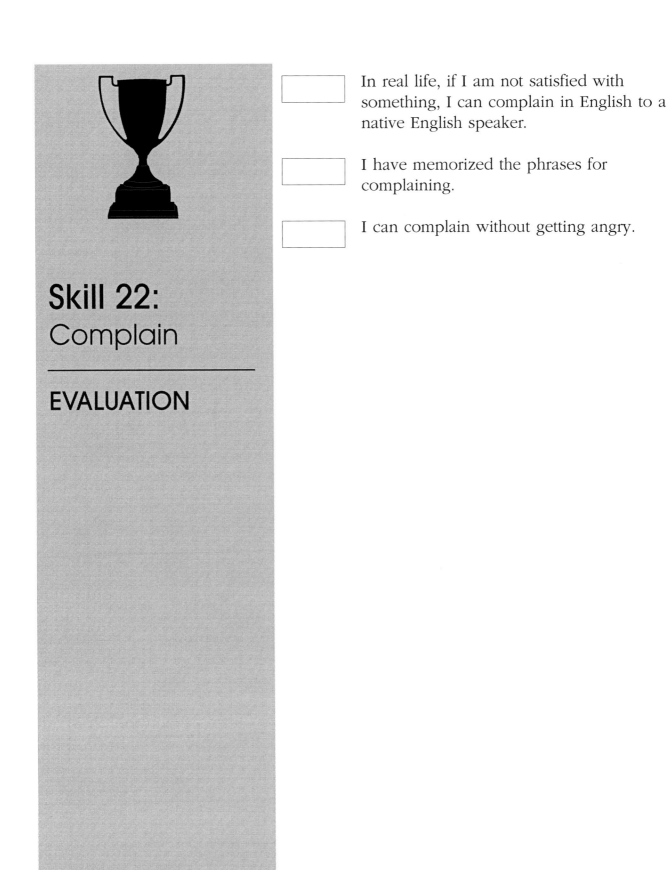

☐ In real life, if I am not satisfied with something, I can complain in English to a native English speaker.

☐ I have memorized the phrases for complaining.

☐ I can complain without getting angry.

Skill 23: Lead a meeting

Skill 23:
Lead a meeting

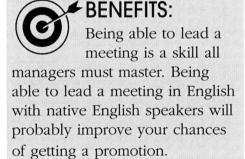 **GOALS:**
Lead a meeting. Say the purpose of the meeting at the beginning. Ask for opinions. Make sure everyone has a chance to speak. Determine the general opinion of the group. Conclude the meeting and thank everyone for coming.

BENEFITS:
Being able to lead a meeting is a skill all managers must master. Being able to lead a meeting in English with native English speakers will probably improve your chances of getting a promotion.

 **Phrases:**

Lets get started.
The purpose of this meeting is to....(purpose)
As you know....(background information)

First, well talk about... (agenda item)
Next, well talk about...(agenda item)
Finally, well decide...(agenda item)

What do you think?
Do you agree?
Does anyone have anything else to say?
Are there any other comments?

How many people think we should...
OK, lets vote. Everyone who thinks we should _____ please raise your hand.

We have decided to...(decision)

This meeting is finished. Thank you for coming.

PERFORMANCE 23.1

Your teacher will give you a topic. Take turns leading the meeting.

PERFORMANCE 23.2

Your teacher will give you a topic. Take turns leading the meeting. Your teacher will join in the meeting, but will talk about the same thing for too long. Rephrase your teachers opinion (Skill 19) to force your teacher to stop talking. This will give the other participants more opportunity to share their opinions.

Skill 23:
Lead a meeting

EVALUATION

	I have memorized the phrases for leading a meeting.
	Even if a meeting is tense and many native English speakers seem angry, I will be able to remember the phrases I memorized.
	I can begin each meeting by saying the purpose of the meeting.
	I give everyone an opportunity to add his or her opinions.
	I remember how to rephrase someones opinion (Skill 19).
	At the end of a meeting, I can clearly summarize what was decided.

Skill 24: Make a presentation

Skill 24:
Make a presentation

GOALS:
Stand in front of people and make a presentation. Have eye contact with everyone in the room. Be energetic. Memorize about half of your presentation, and read the other half. Memorize and use the phrases shown below in order to make a presentation with a very clear structure.

BENEFITS:
You will be able to present information in a way native English speakers will find easy to understand. You will make a good impression for yourself and for your company.

Phrases: (question)

Today, I'll talk about.....
(presentation topic, summary of entire presentation)
First, I'll talk about.... (1st main point)
Next, I'll talk about... (2nd main point)
Finally, I'll talk about... (3rd main point)
Then, if you have any questions, I'll be happy to answer them.

Phrases: (body)

First, I'll talk about.... (details of the 1st main point)
Next, I'll talk about... (details of the 2nd main point)
Finally, I'll talk about... (details of the 3rd main point)

Phrases: (conclusion)

Today I talked about...(presentation topic)
As you can see, (main summary of presentation)
First, I talked about.... (details of the 1st main point)
Next, I talked about... (details of the 2nd main point)
Finally, I talked about... (details of the 3rd main point)

Example:
(teacher presentation)

PERFORMANCE 24.1

Make a very simple three-minute presentation about your favorite restaurant. Use all the phrases in this lesson. First practice your speech in front of a classmate. Then give your speech to the entire class.

Skill 24:
Make a presentation

EVALUATION

☐ My presentation is about half memorized. I memorized half and read half.

☐ I make eye contact with everyone in the room when I speak to them.

☐ I speak loudly and clearly.

☐ I have memorized the phrases used for making a presentation with clear structure.

☐ The pace of my speaking is fast enough that native English speakers won't get bored.

☐ I am energetic when I give a presentation.

Skill 25: Lead a question and answer session

Skill 25:
Lead a question and answer session

Phrases:

GOALS:
After giving a presentation, ask for and answer questions from the audience. Control the conversation. Make a good impression. Do not show nervousness. Answer all the questions, or suggest other ways people can find the answers.

BENEFITS:
The audience will be able to understand your presentation better if they can ask questions. You will be less nervous in giving the speech if you are confident that you will be able to lead the question and answer session afterwards.

If you have any questions, I'll be happy to answer them.

Are there any questions?

Does that answer your question?

Are there any other questions?

I don't have an answer to that question right now. Let me get back to you later with an answer.

If there are no other questions, I will stop here.

Thank you very much for your time.

PERFORMANCE 25.1

Give a very simple three-minute presentation about what you did last weekend. Use the phrases you memorized in Skill 24. After your presentation is finished, answer any questions the audience has.

PERFORMANCE 25.2

Give a simple five-minute presentation about your hometown. Answer questions after your speech.

PERFORMANCE 25.3

Give a seven-minute presentation about your job. Answer questions after your speech.

Skill 25: Lead a question and answer session

EVALUATION

☐ I can lead a question and answer session with several native English speakers.

☐ I have memorized the phrases necessary for leading a question and answer session.

☐ Even if I am nervous, I will be able to remember the phrases.

☐ I answer questions loudly and clearly.

☐ I look the audience in the eye when I answer questions.

LISTENING SECTION

SKILL 1 – LISTENING
Control a conversation

As you listen, write down the complete sentences for numbers one through four. You may have to listen to each exercise several times. You may not be able to write the sentence completely. The important thing is to understand how the man and woman use the phrases from Skill 1 to control a conversation.

1. _____

_____

_____

2. _____

_____

_____

3. _____

_____

_____

4. _____

_____

_____

SKILL 2 – LISTENING
Start a conversation

Take notes as you listen to the speakers. You may have to listen to each exercise several times. If the speaker talks quickly, you may not be able to understand everything. Get as much information as you can.

1. _____
_____
_____

2. _____
_____
_____

3. _____
_____
_____

4. _____
_____
_____

5. _____
_____
_____

6. _____

_____

_____

7. _____

_____

_____

8. _____

_____

_____

9. _____

_____

_____

10. _____

_____

_____

Listen again. Match the speakers you hear with the descriptions below. The first one is done for you.

(   ) George Biwer, Miyuki Jacobs Hospital, paramedic, St. Louis, wife, swimming

(   ) David Chalberg, Hawaiian Superconductor Incorporated, programmer, Honolulu, wife, tennis

(   ) Sarah Kasper, George Milton High School, math teacher, Joliet, husband and two daughters, scuba diving

(   ) Steven Rogers, American Nursing Corporation, medical administrator, Los Angeles, wife and one son, golf

(   ) Carol Cunningham, Newport Conveyor Company, project engineer, Virginia, husband, reading

(   ) James Townsend, Luxurious Law Associates, lawyer, Miami, son, computer games

(1) Wendy Lin, Knapp Asset Management, research analyst, Washington D.C., husband and two sons, cooking

(   ) Mary Packard, First Bank of Eastern Florida, customer service representative, Orlando, husband, fishing

(   ) Gloria Lynch, Jimmy Smart Title Company, administrative assistant, Seattle, mother and father, gardening

(   ) Randy Tolentino, United Peach Truck Lines, truck driver, San Francisco, wife and daughter, watching TV

SKILL 3 – LISTENING
Introduce yourself

Take notes as you listen to the speakers. You may have to listen to each exercise several times. Sometimes the man speaks quickly. You may not be able to understand everything. Get as much information as you can.

1. _____

    _____

    _____

2. _____

    _____

    _____

3. _____

    _____

    _____

4. _____

    _____

    _____

5. _____

    _____

    _____

6. _____

_____

_____

7. _____

_____

_____

8. _____

_____

_____

9. _____

_____

_____

10. _____

_____

_____

Listen again. Match the speakers you hear with the descriptions below.

(   )   Terri Ziemba, Turvey Management Resources, legal secretary, Nashville, husband and three children, skiing

(   )   John Bowers, Chowder Memorial Hospital, doctor, Toronto, wife and daughter, hiking

(   )   Jane Cahill, Thornwood Department Stores, sales associate, Springfield, mother and daughter, playing with my daughter

(   )   Gary Lawless, Red Cone Software, training coordinator, Dallas, wife, listening to music

(   )   Dana Rensi, Hillcrest Sims Associates, accountant, Atlanta, husband and daughter, playing the piano

(   )   Richard Speta, Douglas Middaugh Manufacturing, marketing manager, Jacksonville, wife, shopping

(   )   Julie Kraska, Hoffman Brookbank Incorporated, environmental attorney, Boston, husband and three sons, going to the movies

(   )   Mark Kresl, Green Pixy Finance, account executive, New York, wife and father, going to the theater

(   )   Stacey Priest, Blurry Vision Associates, graphic designer, Detroit, husband, watching videos

(   )   Matthew Neverly, Blue Oak Hospital, nurse, Baltimore, wife and two sons, playing sports with my children

SKILL 4 – LISTENING
Describe your job and your company

Take notes as you listen to the speakers. You may have to listen to each exercise several times. If the speaker talks quickly, you may not be able to understand everything. Get as much information as you can.

1. _____

_____

_____

2. _____

_____

_____

3. _____

_____

_____

4. _____

_____

_____

5. _____

_____

_____

6. _____

_____

_____

7. _____

_____

_____

8. _____

_____

_____

9. _____

_____

_____

10. _____

_____

_____

Listen again. Match the speakers you hear with the descriptions below.

( )   1984, gardening tools, home gardeners, Paris, 5 factories in France, 3 factories in other countries, 392 employees, 17 people work in the head office, Carol West, 128,579,000 euros (2001)

( )   1897, railway equipment, large railway companies, London, 2 factories in England, 3 factories in other countries, 239 employees, 59 people work in the head office, Donald Kimberly, 458,975,543,000 pounds (1999)

( )   1901, computer monitors, computer system manufacturers, Hong Kong, 2 factories in Hong Kong, 3 factories in other countries, 398 employees, 45 people work in the head office, Jacob Bala, 385,295,000 Hong Kong Dollars (2001)

( )   1945, soap and shampoo, single women between the ages of 18 and 39, Phoenix, 1 factory in the United States, 3 factories in other countries, 873 employees, 84 people work in the head office, Bill Machuga, $238,296,000,000 (2002)

( )   1950, women's and children's clothing, families on a tight budget, Bangkok, 12 factories in Thailand, 2 factories in other countries, 981 employees, 56 people work in the head office, William Rock, 456,789,000,000 Thai Bhat (2001)

( )   1925, aircraft parts, large airlines, Chicago, 1 factory in the United States, 2 factories in other countries, 285 employees, 12 people work in the head office, Kathy Green, $237,293,000 (2001)

( )   1852, clocks and watches, wealthy individuals, Milan, 1 factory in Italy, no factories in other countries, 23 employees, 5 people work in the head office, Eric Luxow, 223,000 Lira (1999)

( )   2001, fiber optic switches, telecommunication companies, Seattle, 2 factories in the United States, 2 factories in other countries, 512 employees, 45 people work in the head office, Gary Niemietz, $295,739,205 (2002)

( )   1987, animal vaccines, zoos, Denver, 1 factory in the United States, 4 factories in other countries, 156 employees, 56 people work in the head office, John Routbort, $129,152,000 (2001)

( )   1965, two-way radios and handheld electronics, law enforcement agencies, New York, 2 factories in the United States, no factories in other countries, 193 employees, 23 people work in the head office, James Tedroe, $235,306,000 (2002)

SKILL 5 – LISTENING
Use large and small numbers

Write the information for each company. The man sometimes talks very quickly. Can you understand everything he says?

annual sales
total expenses
gross profit
profit margin
number of employees

1. _____

2. _____

3. _____

4. _____

SKILL 6 – Listening
Exchange company data

Write the information for each company.

company
address
phone number
annual sales
number of employees

1. _____

2. _____

3. _____

4. _____

SKILL 8 – LISTENING
Take or leave a telephone message

Write the information for each phone call. You may have to listen to each phone call more than once.

	Caller's Name	Company	Telephone Number
1.	_____	_____	_____
2.	_____	_____	_____
3.	_____	_____	_____
4.	_____	_____	_____

SKILL 11 – LISTENING
Making an appointment

Listen and write the meeting time, day and place.

	Time	Day	Place
1.	_____	_____	_____
2.	_____	_____	_____
3.	_____	_____	_____
4.	_____	_____	_____
5.	_____	_____	_____
6.	_____	_____	_____

SKILL 18 – LISTENING
Ask for, give and support an opinion

Circle the preferred choice. Write the reason that supports the opinion.

1. plastic / wood

   _____

   _____

2. flying to New York / taking the train

   _____

   _____

3. increasing the price / lowering the quality

   _____

   _____

4. Mr. Smith / Mr. Jones

   _____

   _____

5. firing 3 employees / raising our prices

   _____

   _____

6. Ms. Douglas / Ms. Parker

   _____

   _____

LISTENING SECTION ANSWERS

SKILL 1 LISTENING ANSWERS

1. For the third time this summer, the Federal Power Authority has asked its customers to reduce electricity use to prevent power disruptions in light of the recent high heat and humidity.

2. The average price of land dropped for the 12th straight year, down 7.3% to $250 per square foot.

3. A masked man armed with what appeared to be a hunting rifle robbed farmer Walter Brubaker of $13,000 and took his 19-year-old daughter, Amanda, hostage in central Kansas Friday evening.

4. For the fiscal year ended December 31, 2001, revenues rose 1.7% to $2.93 billion and net income fell 59% to $61.8 million.

SKILL 2 LISTENING ANSWERS

(4) George Biwer, Miyuki Jacobs Hospital, paramedic, St. Louis, wife, swimming

(2) David Chalberg, Hawaiian Superconductor Incorporated, programmer, Honolulu, wife, tennis

(3) Sarah Kasper, George Milton High School, math teacher, Joliet, husband and two daughters, scuba diving

(8) Steven Rogers, American Nursing Corporation, medical administrator, Los Angeles, wife and one son, golf

(5) Carol Cunningham, Newport Conveyor Company, project engineer, Virginia, husband, reading

(6) James Townsend, Luxurious Law Associates, lawyer, Miami, son, computer games

(1) Wendy Lin, Knapp Asset Management, research analyst, Washington D.C., husband and two sons, cooking

(9) Mary Packard, First Bank of Eastern Florida, customer service representative, Orlando, husband, fishing

(7) Gloria Lynch, Jimmy Smart Title Company, administrative assistant, Seattle, mother and father, gardening

(10) Randy Tolentino, United Peach Truck Lines, truck driver, San Francisco, wife and daughter, watching TV

SKILL 3 LISTENING ANSWERS

(5) Terri Ziemba, Turvey Management Resources, legal secretary, Nashville, husband and three children, skiing

(2) John Bowers, Chowder Memorial Hospital, doctor, Toronto, wife and daughter, hiking

(1) Jane Cahill, Thornwood Department Stores, sales associate, Springfield, mother and daughter, playing with my daughter

(4) Gary Lawless, Red Cone Software, training coordinator, Dallas, wife, listening to music

(7) Dana Rensi, Hillcrest Sims Associates, accountant, Atlanta, husband and daughter, playing the piano

(10) Richard Speta, Douglas Middaugh Manufacturing, marketing manager, Jacksonville, wife, shopping

(3) Julie Kraska, Hoffman Brookbank Incorporated, environmental attorney, Boston, husband and three sons, going to the movies

(6) Mark Kresl, Green Pixy Finance, account executive, New York, wife and father, going to the theater

(9) Stacey Priest, Blurry Vision Associates, graphic designer, Detroit, husband, watching videos

(8) Matthew Neverly, Blue Oak Hospital, nurse, Baltimore, wife and two sons, playing sports with my children

SKILL 4 LISTENING ANSWERS

(9) 1984, gardening tools, home gardeners, Paris, 5 factories in France, 3 factories in other countries, 392 employees, 17 people work in the head office, Carol West, 128,579,000 euros (2001)

(1) 1897, railway equipment, large railway companies, London, 2 factories in England, 3 factories in other countries, 239 employees, 59 people work in the head office, Donald Kimberly, 458,975,543,000 pounds (1999)

(10) 1901, computer monitors, computer system manufacturers, Hong Kong, 2 factories in Hong Kong, 3 factories in other countries, 398 employees, 45 people work in the head office, Jacob Bala, 385,295,000 Hong Kong Dollars (2001)

(2) A1945, soap and shampoo, single women between the ages of 18 and 39, Phoenix, 1 factory in the United States, 3 factories in other countries, 873 employees, 84 people work in the head office, Bill Machuga, $238,296,000,000 (2002)

(8) 1950, women's and children's clothing, families on a tight budget, Bangkok, 12 factories in Thailand, 2 factories in other countries, 981 employees, 56 people work in the head office, William Rock, 456,789,000,000 Thai Bhat (2001)

(6) 1925, aircraft parts, large airlines, Chicago, 1 factory in the United States, 2 factories in other countries, 285 employees, 12 people work in the head office, Kathy Green, $237,293,000 (2001)

(3) 1852, clocks and watches, wealthy individuals, Milan, 1 factory in Italy, no factories in other countries, 23 employees, 5 people work in the head office, Eric Luxow, 223,000 Lira (1999)

(7) 2001, fiber optic switches, telecommunication companies, Seattle, 2 factories in the United States, 2 factories in other countries, 512 employees, 45 people work in the head office, Gary Niemietz, $295,739,205 (2002)

(5) 1987, animal vaccines, zoos, Denver, 1 factory in the United States, 4 factories in other countries, 156 employees, 56 people work in the head office, John Routbort, $129,152,000 (2001)

(4) 1965, two-way radios and handheld electronics, law enforcement agencies, New York, 2 factories in the United States, no factories in other countries, 193 employees, 23 people work in the head office, James Tedroe, $235,306,000 (2002)

SKILL 5 LISTENING ANSWERS

1. 195,529,873,239 dollars
    154,295,397,019 dollars
    41,234,476,220 dollars
    21.08%
    56,846

2. 465,215,684,160 bhat
    367,486,016,259 bhat
    97,729,667,901 bhat
    21.007%
    12,238

3. 976,970,171,897 won
    871,976,497,189 won
    104,993,674,708 won
    10.74%
    25,195

4. 704,980,197,049 yen
    681,684,049,681 yen
    23,296,147,368 yen
    3.304%
    35,239

SKILL 6 LISTENING ANSWERS

1. April Green Bicycles
   3968 Milwaukee Avenue
   Sherman Oaks, NY 62395
   297-456-0145
   $173,214,265,000
   150,515 employees

2. Sparrow Turner Electric
   3135 Grant Street
   Fairview, CT 85267
   298-540-0450
   $125,967,489,000
   284,955 employees

3. Catfish Signal Group Services
   7206 North Sport Lane
   Summer Grove, CA 08571
   595-238-2121
   $121,814,384,273
   236,702 employees

4. Dark Cloud Financial
   One Dark Cloud Center
   Miami, FL 39264
   497-206-3747
   $38,657,748,275
   57,640 employees

SKILL 8 – LISTENING ANSWERS

	Caller's Name	Company	Telephone Number
1.	Sandy Simpson	Brass Quarter Securities	395-150-1567
2.	Jeff Miller	Burlington Fenton Bank	996-408-5434
3.	Kim Wrobel	Alpha Carp Incorporated	890-058-5605
4.	Peter Holpuck	Moore Robin Finance	697-465-4500

SKILL 11 – LISTENING ANSWERS

	Time	Day	Place
1.	5:00	Monday	on the first floor
2.	7:30 p.m.	Friday	in front of the New York Stock Exchange
3.	Noon	Wednesday	Starbucks
4.	6:00 p.m.	Thursday	hotel lobby
5.	7:00 a.m.	Sunday	golf course parking lot
6.	11:00 a.m.	Saturday	Seoul train station, in front of the newspaper stand

SKILL 18 – LISTENING ANSWERS

1. (plastic)/ wood – Plastic is cheaper.
2. (flying to New York)/taking the train – Flying is faster.
3. increasing the price/(lowering the quality) – Customer prefer lower prices.
4. Mr. Smith/(Mr. Jones) – Mr. Smith lacks technical knowledge about our industry.
5. (firing 3 employees)/raising our prices – Our products are already too expensive.
6. Ms. Douglas/ (Ms. Parker) – Ms. Parker has contributed more to our company.

CD TRANSCRIPT

Track 1

Track 2 -
Skill I: Control a conversation. - Number 1

W: For the third time this summer, the Federal. ...

M: Excuse me, could you say that again from the beginning?

W: For the third time this summer, the Federal Power. ...

M: Excuse me, how do you spell Federal?

W: Federal is spelled capital f-e-d-e-r-a-l.

M: OK, let me make sure I understand. You said "Federal is spelled capital f-e-d-e-r-a-l." Is that correct?

W: Yes, that's correct.

M: Could you say that again from the beginning?

W: For the third time this summer, the Federal Power Authority has asked its customers to reduce electricity use. ...

M: Excuse me, let me make sure I understand. You said "the Federal Power Authority has asked its customers." Is that correct?

W: Yes, that's correct.

M: What did you say after customers?

W: ... to reduce electricity use to prevent power disruptions. ...

M: Excuse me, what did you say after power?

W: Disruptions.

M: I'm sorry. How do you spell disruptions?

W: Disruptions is spelled d-i-s-r-u-p-t-i-o-n-s.

M: OK, let me make sure I understand. You said, "disruptions is spelled d-i-s-r-u-p-t-i-o-n-s." Is that correct?

W: Yes, that's correct.

M: Excuse me, what does power disruptions mean?

W: Power disruptions means blackouts.

M: Oh, OK. Eh, let me make sure I understand. You said, "For the third time this summer, the Federal Power Authority has asked its customers to reduce electricity use to prevent power disruptions." Is that correct?

W: Yes, that's correct.

M: OK. Please continue.

W: ... to prevent power disruptions in light of the recent high heat and humidity.

M: I'm sorry, how do you spell humidity?

W: Humidity is spelled h-u-m-i-d-i-t-y.

M: OK, let me make sure I understand. You said "Humidity is spelled h-u-m-i-d-i-t-y." Is that correct?

W: Yes, that's correct.

M: OK, let me make sure I understand. You said, "For the third time this summer, the Federal Power Authority has asked its customers to reduce electricity use to prevent power disruptions in light of the recent high heat and humidity." Is that correct?

W: Yes, that's correct.

Track 3 - Number 2

M: The average price of land dropped. ...

W: Excuse me, could you say that again more slowly?

M: Uh-huh. The average price of land dropped for the 12th straight year. ...

W: Excuse me, what did you say before for?

M: Ah...the average price of land dropped.

W: How do you spell dropped?

M: Dropped is spelled d-r-o-p-p-e-d.

W: Let me make sure I understand. You said "Dropped is spelled d-r-o-p-p-e-d." Is that correct?

M: Yes, that's correct.

W: What does dropped mean?

M: Dropped means fell or went lower.

W: Thank you. Please continue.

M: The average price of land dropped for the 12th straight year, down 7.3% to $250 per square foot.

W: I'm sorry, could you say that again, please?

M: Uh-huh. The average price of land dropped for the 12th straight year, down 7.3%...

W: Excuse me, what did you say after 7.3?

M: 7.3%.

W: Thank you. Please continue.

M: ... 7.3% to $250 per square foot.

W: What did you say before foot?

M: Eh, square.

W: How do you spell square?

M: Square is spelled s-q-u-a-r-e.

W: Can you say that again from the beginning, please?

M: Uh-huh. The average price of land dropped for the 12th straight year, down 7.3% to $250 per square foot.

W: Let me make sure I understand. You said "The average price of land dropped for the 12th straight year, down 7.5% to $250 per square foot." Is that correct?

M: No, no, no. I said "down 7.3% to $250 per square foot."

W: OK, let me make sure I understand. You said "The average price of land dropped for the 12th straight year, down 7.3% to $250 per square foot." Is that correct?

M: Yes, that's correct.

Track 4 – Number 3

W: A masked man armed with what appeared....

M: Excuse me, could you say that again from the beginning?

W: A masked man....

M: Excuse me, what did you say before man?

W: Masked.

M: I'm sorry, how do you spell masked?

W: Masked is spelled m-a-s-k-e-d.

M: Eh, OK. Let me make sure I understand. You said "Masked is spelled m-a-s-k-e-d?" Is that correct?

W: Yes, that's correct.

M: Excuse me, what does masked mean?

W: Masked means wearing a mask.

M: Oh, OK. Could you say that again from the beginning?

W: A masked man armed with what appeared to be a hunting rifle robbed farmer Walter Brubaker....

M: I'm sorry. Could you say that again more slowly?

W: A masked man armed with what appeared to be a hunting rifle robbed farmer Walter Brubaker....

M: Excuse me, how do you spell Brubaker?

W: Brubaker is spelled capital b-r-u-b-a-k-e-r.

M: OK, let me make sure I understand. You said, "Brubaker is spelled capital b-r-u-b-a-k-e-r." Is that correct?

W: Yes, that's correct.

M: Ah, OK. Please continue.

W: ... Walter Brubaker of $13,000 and took his 19-year-old daughter, Amanda...

M: Excuse me. Ah, what did you say after daughter?

W: Amanda.

M: I'm sorry. How do you spell Amanda?

W: Amanda is spelled capital a-m-a-n-d-a.

M: OK, let me make sure I understand. You said Amanda is spelled capital a-m-a-n-d-a. Is that correct?

W: Yes, that's correct.

M: OK, please continue.

W: ... hostage in central Kansas Friday evening.

M: I'm sorry, could you say that again? What did you say after Amanda?

W: Hostage.

M: I'm sorry, how do you spell hostage?

W: Hostage is spelled h-o-s-t-a-g-e.

M: OK, let me make sure I understand. You said "Hostage is spelled h-o-s-t-a-g-e." Is that correct?

W: Yes, that's correct.

M: OK, what did you say after hostage?

W: ... in central Kansas Friday evening.

M: OK, let me make sure I understand. You said "A masked man armed with what appeared to be a hunting rifle robbed farmer Walter Brubaker of $13,000 and took his 19-year-old daughter, Amanda, hostage in central..." I'm sorry, what did you say after central?

W: Kansas.

M: Ah, I'm sorry, how do you spell Kansas?

W: Kansas is spelled capital k-a-n-s-a-s.

M: OK, let me make sure I understand. You said "Kansas is spelled capital k-a-n-s-a-s." Is that correct?

W: Yes, that's correct.

M: OK, let me make sure I understand. You said, "A masked man armed with what appeared to be a hunting rifle robbed farmer Walter Brubaker of $13,000 and took his 19-year-old daughter, Amanda, hostage in central Kansas Friday evening." Is that correct?

W: Yes, that's correct.

Track 5 – Number 4

M: For the fiscal year ended December 31....

W: Excuse me, could you say that again more slowly.

M: Sure. For the fiscal year ended December....

W: Excuse me, what did you say before year?

M: Fiscal.

W: How do you spell fiscal?

M: Fiscal is spelled f-i-s-c-a-l.

W: Let me make sure I understand. You said, "Fiscal is spelled f-i-s-c-a-l." Is that correct?

M: Yes, that's correct.

W: Please continue.

M: ... fiscal year ended December 31, 2001, revenues rose 1 point....

W: Excuse me.

M: Ah-huh?

W: What did you say before rose?

M: Revenues.

W: What does revenues mean?

M: Revenues is money that a company gets. It's like income.

W: How do you spell revenues?

M: Revenues is spelled r-e-v-e-n-u-e-s.

W: Let me make sure I understand. You said, "Revenues is spelled r-e-b-e-n-u-e-s." Is that correct?

M: No, that isn't correct. Revenues is spelled r-e-v-e-n-u-e-s.

W: Let me make sure I understand. You said, "Revenues is spelled r-e-v-e-n-u-e-s." Is that correct?

M: Yes, that's correct.

W: Please continue.

M: ... revenues rose 1.7% to $2.93 billon dollars and net income fell...

W: Could you say that again more clearly?

M: Mm-huh. … revenues rose 1.7% to $2.93 billon dollars and net income fell…

W: Excuse me, what did you say after net?

M: Net income. …net income fell 59% to $61.8 million dollars.

W: Excuse me, how do you spell income?

M: Income is spelled i-n-c-o-m-e.

W: What did you say after income?

M: …income fell 59% to $61.8 million dollars.

W: Let me make sure I understand. You said, "Income is spelled i-n-c-o-m-e." Is that correct?

M: Yes, that's correct.

W: And you said that net income fell 59% to $61.8 million dollars. Is that correct?

M: Yes, that's correct.

W: OK. Could you say that again from the beginning?

M: Mm-huh. For the fiscal year ended December 31, 2001, revenues rose 1.7% to $2.93 billion dollars and net income fell 59% to $61.8 million dollars.

W: Let me make sure I understand. You said, "For the fiscal year ended December 31, 2001, revenues rose 1.7% to $2.93 billion dollars and net income fell 59% to $61.8 million dollars." Is that correct?

M: Yes, that's correct.

Track 6 -
Skill 2: Start a conversation - Number 1

M: Hello, my name is Joe Smith.

W: My name is Wendy Lin.

M: It's nice to meet you.

W: It's nice to meet you too.

M: Who do you work for?

W: I work for Knapp Asset Management.

M: Hmm, what do you do?

W: I'm a research analyst.

M: Where do you live?

W: I live in Washington D.C.

M: Do you have a family?

W: Yes, there are four people in my family: my husband and my two sons and I.

M: What do you like to do in your free time?

W: I like cooking.

M: Well, it was nice meeting you.

W: It was nice meeting you too.

M: Good-bye.

W: Good-bye.

Track 7 - Number 2

W: Hello, my name is Mary Smith.

M: My name is David Chalberg.

W: It's nice to meet you.

M: It's nice to meet you too.

W: Who do you work for?

M: I work for Hawaiian Superconductor Incorporated.

W: What do you do?

M: I'm a programmer.

W: Where do you live?

M: I live in Honolulu.

W: Do you have a family?

M: Yes, there are two people in my family: my wife and I.

W: What do you like to do in your free time?

M: I like playing tennis.

W: Well, it was nice meeting you.

M: It was nice meeting you too.

W: Good-bye.

M: Good-bye.

Track 8 - Number 3

M: Hello, my name is Joe Smith.

W: My name is Sarah Kasper.

M: It's nice to meet you.

W: It's nice to meet you too.

M: Who do you work for?

W: I work for George Milton High School.

M: Ah, what do you do?

W: I'm a math teacher.

M: Where do you live?

W: I live in Joliet.

M: Do you have a family?

W: Yes, there are four people in my family: my husband, my two daughters and I.

M: What do you like to do in your free time?

W: I like scuba diving.

M: Well, it was nice meeting you.

W: It was nice meeting you too.

M: Good-bye.

W: Good-bye.

Track 9 - Number 4

W: Hello, my name is Mary Smith.

M: My name is George Biwer.

W: It's nice to meet you.

M: It's nice to meet you too.

W: Who do you work for?

M: I work for Miyuki Jacobs Hospital.

W: What do you do?

M: I'm a Paramedic

W: Where do you live?

M: I live in St. Louis.

W: Do you have a family?

M: Yes, there are two people in my family: my wife and I.

W: What do you like to do in your free time?
M: I like swimming.
W: Well, it was nice meeting you.
M: It was nice meeting you too.
W: Good-bye.
M: Good-bye.

Track 10 - Number 5

M: Hello, my name is Joe Smith.
W: My name is Carol Cunningham.
M: It's nice to meet you.
W: It's nice to meet you too.
M: Who do you work for?
W: I work for Newport Conveyor Company.
M: What do you do?
W: I'm a project engineer.
M: Where do you live?
W: I live in Virginia.
M: Do you have a family?
W: Yes, there are two people in my family: my husband and I.
M: What do you like to do in your free time?
W: I like reading.
M: Well, it was nice meeting you.
W: It was nice meeting you too.
M: Good-bye.
W: Good-bye.

Track 11 - Number 6

W: Hello, my name is Mary Smith.
M: My name is James Townsend.
W: It's nice to meet you.
M: It's nice to meet you too.
W: Who do you work for?
M: I work for Luxurious Law Associates.
W: Oh, what do you do?
M: I'm a lawyer.
W: Where do you live?
M: I live in Miami.
W: Do you have a family?
M: Yes, there are two people in my family: my son and I.
W: What do you like to do in your free time?
M: I like playing computer games.
W: Well, it was nice meeting you.
M: It was nice meeting you too.
W: Good-bye.
M: Good-bye.

Track 12 - Number 7

M: Hello, my name is Joe Smith.
W: My name's Gloria Lynch.
M: It's nice to meet you.

W: It's nice to meet you too.
M: Who do you work for?
W: I work for Jimmy Smart Title Company.
M: What do you do?
W: I'm an administrative assistant.
M: Where do you live?
W: I live in Seattle.
M: Do you have a family?
W: Yes, there are three people in my family: my mother, my father and I.
M: What do you like to do in your free time?
W: I like gardening.
M: Well, it was nice meeting you.
W: It was nice meeting you too.
M: Good-bye.
W: Good-bye.

Track 13 - Number 8

W: Hello, my name is Mary Smith.
M: My name is Steven Rogers.
W: It's nice to meet you.
M: It's nice to meet you too.
W: Who do you work for?
M: I work for American Nursing Corporation.
W: Oh, what do you do?
M: I'm a medical administrator.
W: Where do you live?
M: I live in Los Angeles.
W: Do you have a family?
M: Yes, there are three people in my family: my wife, my son and I.
W: What do you like to do in your free time?
M: I like playing golf.
W: Well, it was nice meeting you.
M: It was nice meeting you too.
W: Good-bye.
M: Good-bye.

Track 14 - Number 9

M: Hello, my name is Joe Smith.
W: My name is Mary Packard.
M: It's nice to meet you.
W: It's nice to meet you too.
M: Who do you work for?
W: I work for the First Bank of Eastern Florida.
M: What do you do?
W: I'm customer service representative.
M: Where do you live?
W: I live in Orlando.
M: Do you have a family?
W: Yes, there are two people in my family: my husband and I.

M: What do you like to do in your free time?
W: I like fishing.
M: Well, it was nice meeting you.
W: It was nice meeting you too.
M: Good-bye.
W: Good-bye.

Track 15 - Number 10

W: Hello, my name is Mary Smith.
M: My name is Randy Tolentino.
W: It's nice to meet you.
M: It's nice to meet you too.
W: Who do you work for?
M: I work for United Peach Truck Lines.
W: What do you do?
M: I'm a truck driver.
W: Where do you live?
M: I live in San Francisco.
W: Do you have a family?
M: Yes, there are three people in my family: my wife, my daughter and I.
W: What do you like to do in your free time?
M: I like watching TV.
W: Well, it was nice meeting you.
M: It was nice meeting you too.
W: Good-bye.
M: Good-bye.

Track 16 -
Skill 3: Introduce yourself - Number 1

My name is Jane Cahill. I work for Thornwood Department Stores. I'm a sales associate. I live in Springfield. There are three people in my family: my mother, my daughter and I. I like playing with my daughter in my free time.

Track 17 - Number 2

My name is John Bowers. I work for Chowder Memorial Hospital. I'm a doctor. I live in Toronto. There are three people in my family: my wife, my daughter and I. I like hiking in my free time.

Track 18 - Number 3

Hello. My name is Julie Kraska. I work for Hoffman Brookbank Incorporated.
I'm an environmental attorney. I live in Boston. There are five people in my family: my husband, our three sons and I. I like going to the movies in my free time.

Track 19 - Number 4

Good morning. My name is Gary Lawless. I work for Red Cone Software. I'm a training coordinator. I live in Dallas. There are two people in my family: my wife and I. I like listening to music in my free time.

Track 20 - Number 5

My name is Terri Ziemba. I work for Turvey Management Resources. I'm a legal secretary. I live in Nashville. There are five people in my family: my husband, our three children and I. I like skiing in my free time.

Track 21 - Number 6

My name is Mark Kresl. I work for Green Pixy Finance. I'm an account executive. I live in New York. There are three people in my family: my wife, my father and I. I like going to the theater in my free time.

Track 22 - Number 7

Good afternoon. My name is Dana Rensi. I work for Hillcrest Sims Associates. I'm an accountant. I live in Atlanta. There are three people in my family: my husband, our daughter and I. I like playing the piano in my free time.

Track 23 - Number 8

Hello. My name is Matthew Neverly. I work for Blue Oak Hospital. I'm a nurse. I live in Baltimore. There are four people in my family: my wife, our two sons and I. I like playing sports with my children in my free time.

Track 24 - Number 9

My name is Stacey Priest. I work for Blurry Vision Associates. I'm a graphic designer. I live in Detroit. There are two people in my family: my husband and I. I like watching videos in my free time.

Track 25 - Number 10

My name is Richard Speta. I work for Douglas Middaugh Manufacturing. I'm a marketing manager. I live in Jacksonville. There are two people in my family, my wife and I. I like shopping in my free time.

CD Transcript

Track 26 -
Skill 4 Describe your job and your company - Number 1

Our company was established in 1897. We produce railway equipment. Our main customers are large railway companies. Our head office is located in London. Our company has two factories in England. We have three factories in other countries. Our company has 239 employees. Fifty-nine people work in the head office. Our company's president's name is Donald Kimberly. Our annual sales were 458,975,543,000 pounds in 1999.

Track 27 - Number 2

Our company was established in 1945. We produce soap and shampoo. Our main customers are single women between the ages of eighteen and thirty-nine. Our head office is located in Phoenix. We have one factory in the United States. Our company has three factories in other countries. Our company has 873 employees. Eighty-four people work in the head office. Our company president is Bill Machuga. Our annual sales were $238,296,000,000 in 2002.

Track 28 - Number 3

Our company was established in 1852. We produce clocks and watches. Our main customers are wealthy individuals. Our head office is located in Milan. We have one factory in Italy. We have no factories in other countries. Our company has twenty-three employees. Five people work in the head office. Eric Lexow is our company's president. Our annual sales were 223,000 Lira in 1999.

Track 29 - Number 4

Our company was established in 1965. We produce two-way radios and handheld electronics. Our main customers are law enforcement agencies. Our head office is located in New York. We have two factories in the United States. We don't have any factories in other countries. Our company has 193 employees. Twenty-three people work in the head office. Our company president is James Tedroe. Our annual sales were $235,306,000 in 2002.

Track 30 - Number 5

Our company was established in 1987. We produce animal vaccines. Our main customers are zoos. Our head office is located in Denver. We have one factory in the United States. We have four factories in other countries.

Our company has 156 employees. Fifty-six people work in our head office. John Routbort is our company's president. Our annual sales were $129,152,000 in 2001.

Track 31 - Number 6

Our company was established in 1925. We produce aircraft parts. Our main customers are large airlines. Our company's head office is located in Chicago. We have one factory in the United States. Our company has two factories in other countries. Our company has 285 employees. Twelve people work in the head office. Kathy Green is our company's president. Our annual sales were $237,293,000 in 2001.

Track 32 - Number 7

Our company was established in 2001. Our company produces fiber optic switches. Our main customers are telecommunication companies. Our head office is located in Seattle. We have two factories in the United States. Our company has two factories in other countries. Our company has 512 employees. Forty-five people work in our head office. Our company president is Gary Niemietz. Our annual sales in 2002 were $295,739,205.

Track 33 - Number 8

Our company was established in 1950. We produce women's and children's clothing. Our main customers are families on a tight budget. Our head office is located in Bangkok. Our company has twelve factories in Thailand. We have two factories in other countries. Our company has 981 employees. Fifty-six people work in the head office. Our company's president's name is William Rock. Our annual sales were 456,789,000,000 Thai Bhat in 2001.

Track 34 - Number 9

Our company was established in 1984. We produce gardening tools. Our main customers are home gardeners. Our head office is located in Paris. We have five factories in France. Our company has three factories in other countries. Our company has 392 employees. Seventeen people work in the head office. Carol West is our company's president. Our annual sales were 128,579,000 euros in 2001.

Track 35 - Number 10

Our company was established in 1901. We produce computer monitors. Our main customers are computer system manufacturers. Our company's head office is located in Hong Kong. We have two factories in Hong Kong. We have three factories in other countries. Our company has 398 employees. Forty-five people work in the head office. Jacob Bala is our company's president. Our annual sales were 385,295,000 Hong Kong Dollars in 2001.

Track 36 -
Skill 5: Use large and small numbers - Number 1

M: How much were your annual sales?

W: Our annual sales were $195,529,873,239.

M: Let me make sure I understand. You said your annual sales were $195,529,873,239. Is that correct?

W: Yes, that's correct.

M: How much were your total expenses?

W: Our total expenses were $154,295,397,019.

M: Let...I'm sorry. Did you say nineteen or ninety?

W: I said nineteen.

M: OK, let me make sure I understand. You said your total expenses were $154,295,397,019. Is that correct?

W: Yes, that's correct.

M: How much was your gross profit?

W: Our gross profit was $41,234,476,220.

M: I'm sorry, what did you say after 476 thousand?

W: 220 dollars.

M: OK, let me make sure I understand. You said your gross profit was $41,234,476,220. Is that correct?

W: Yes, that's correct.

M: How much was your profit margin?

W: Our profit margin was 21.08%.

M: OK, let me make sure I understand. You said your profit margin was 21.08% is that correct?

W: Yes, that's correct.

M: How many employees does your company have?

W: Our company has 56,846 employees.

M: Let me make sure I understand. You said your company has 56,846 employees. Is that correct?

W: Yes, that's correct.

Track 37 - Number 2

W: How much were your annual sales?

M: Our annual sales were 465,215,684,160 bhat.

W: I'm sorry, could you say that again more slowly?

M: Ah-huh. Our annual sales were 465,215,684,160 bhat.

W: Let me make sure I understand. You said that your annual sales were 465,215,684,160 bhat. Is that correct?

M: Yes, that's correct.

W: And how much were your total expenses?

M: Our total expenses were 367,486,016,259 bhat.

W: Could you say that again more clearly?

M: Ah-huh. Our total expenses were 367,486,016,259 bhat.

W: Did you say 16 thousand or 60 thousand?

M: I said 16 thousand.

W: OK, let me make sure I understand. You said your total expenses were 367,486,016,259 bhat. Is that correct?

M: Yes, that's correct.

W: And how much was your gross profit?

M: Our gross profit was 97,729,667,901 bhat.

W: Let me make sure I understand. You said your gross profit was 97,729,667,901 bhat. Is that correct?

M: Yes, that's correct.

W: And how much was your profit margin?

M: Our profit margin was 21.007%.

W: I'm sorry, could you say that again more slowly?

M: Mm-huh. Our profit margin was 21.007%.

W: Let me make sure I understand. You said your profit margin was 21.007% is that correct?

M: Yes, that's correct.

W: And how many employees does your company have?

M: Our company has 12,238 employees.

W: Let me make sure I understand. You said your company has 12,238 employees. Is that correct?

M: Yes, that's correct.

Track 38 - Number 3

M: How much were your annual sales?

W: Our annual sales were 976,970,171,897 won.

M: OK. Let me make sure I understand. You said that your annual sales were 976,970,171,897 won. Is that correct?

W: Yes, that's correct.

M: OK. How much were your total expenses?

W: Our total expenses were 871,976,497,189 won.

M: OK, let me make sure I understand. You said your total expenses were 871,976,497,189 won. Is that correct?

W: Yes, that's correct.

M: How much was your gross profit?

W: Our gross profit was 104,993,674,708 won.

M: I'm sorry, could you say that again?

W: 104,993,674,708 won.

M: OK, let me make sure I understand. You said that your gross profit was 104,993,674,708 won. Is that correct?

W: Yes, that's correct.

M: How much was your profit margin?

W: Our profit margin was 10.74%.

M: Let me make sure I understand. You said your profit margin was 10.74%. Is that correct?

W: Yes, that's correct.

M: How many employees does your company have?

W: Our company has 25,195 employees.

M: OK, let me make sure I understand. You said your company has 25,195 employees. Is that correct?

W: Yes, that's correct.

Track 39 - Number 4

W: How much were your annual sales?

M: Our annual sales were 704,980,197,049 yen.

W: Let me make sure I understand. You said your annual sales were 704,980,197,049 yen. Is that correct?

M: Yes, that's correct.

W: OK. How much were your total expenses?

M: Our total expenses were 681,684,049,681 yen.

W: Let me make sure I understand. You said your total expenses were 682,684,049,681 yen. Is that correct?

M: No, that isn't correct. Our total expenses were 681,684,049,681 yen.

W: OK, let me make sure I understand. You said your total expenses were 681,684,049,681 yen. Is that correct?

M: Yes, that's correct.

W: OK, and how much was your gross profit?

M: Our gross profit was 23,296,147,368 yen.

W: Let me make sure I understand. You said your gross profit was 23,296,147,368 yen. Is that correct?

M: Yes, that's correct.

W: OK. Ah, how much was your profit margin?

M: Our profit margin was 3.304%.

W: Ah, could you please say that again?

M: Uh-huh. Our profit margin was 3.304%.

W: Let me make sure I understand. You said your profit margin was 3.304%. Is that correct?

M: Yes, that's correct.

W: How many employees does your company have?

M: Our company has 35,239 employees.

W: Let me make sure I understand. Your company has 35,239 employees. Is that correct?

M: Yes that's correct.

Track 40 -
Skill 6 - Exchange company data - Number 1

M: Who do you work for?

W: I work for April Green Bicycles.

M: Could I have your address?

W: Our address is 3968 Milwaukee Avenue, Sherman Oaks, NY 62395.

M: What does NY stand for?

W: NY stands for New York.

M: Oh. Could I have your telephone number?

W: Our telephone number is 297-456-0145.

M: How much were your company's annual sales.

W: Our annual sales were $173,214,265,000.

M: How many employees does your company have?

W: Our company has 150,515 employees.

M: I'm sorry, did you say 515 or 550 employees?

W: I said 515 employees.

M: OK, let me make sure I understand. You work for April Green Bicycles. Is that correct?

W: Yes, that's correct.

M: Your address is 3968 Milwaukee Avenue, Sherman Oaks, New York - New York is abbreviated NY-62395. Is that correct?

W: Yes, that's correct.

M: Excuse me, how do you spell Milwaukee?

W: Milwaukee is spelled capital m-i-l-w-a-u-k-e-e.

M: OK, let me make sure I understand. You said "Milwaukee is spelled capital m-i-l-w-a-u-k-e-e." Is that correct?

W: Yes, that's correct.

M: OK. Your telephone number is 297-456-0145. Is that correct?

W: Yes, that's correct.

M: Your annual sales are $173,214,265,000. Is that correct?

W: Yes, that's correct.

M: And you said your company has 150,515 employees. Is that correct?

W: Yes, that's correct.

Track 41 - Number 2

W: Who do you work for?

M: I work for Sparrow Turner Electric.

W: Could I have your address?

M: Mm-huh. Our address is 3135 Grant Street, Fairview, Connecticut 85267.

W: Excuse me. What is the abbreviation for Connecticut?

M: Connecticut is abbreviated capital c capital t.

W: Thank you. Could I have your telephone number?

M: Sure. Our telephone number is 298-540-0450.

W: And how much were your annual sales?

M: Our annual sales were $125,967,489,000.

W: And how many employees does your company have?

M: Our company has 284,955 employees.

W: Let me make sure I understand. You said you work for Sparrow Turner Electric. Is that correct?

M: Yes, that's correct.

W: How do you spell Sparrow?

M: OK. Sparrow is spelled capital s-p-a-r-r-o-w.

W: OK. Let me make sure I understand. You said, "Sparrow is spelled capital s-p-a-r-r-o-w." Is that correct?

M: Yes, that's correct.

W: OK, and your address is 3135 Grant Street, Fairview, Connecticut -and that's abbreviated CT-85267. Is that correct?

M: Yes, that's correct.

W: You said your phone number is 298-540-0450. Is that correct?

M: Yes, that's correct.

W: OK, and let me make sure I understand. You said your annual sales were $125,967,489,000. Is that correct?

M: Yes, that's correct.

W: OK, and you have 284,955 employees. Is that correct?

M: Yes, that's correct.

W: Thank you.

Track 42 - Number 3

M: Who do you work for?

W: I work for Catfish Signal Group.

M: I'm sorry. Could you say that again more slowly?

W: Sure. I work for Catfish Signal Group.

M: Is catfish one word, or two words?

W: Catfish is one word.

M: OK, let me make sure I understand. You said you work for Catfish Signal Group, is that correct?

W: Yes, that's correct.

M: Could I have your address?

W: Sure. Our address is 7206 North Sport Lane....

M: Excuse me. Let me make sure I understand. You said your address is 7206 North Sport Lane, it that correct?

W: Yes, that's correct.

M: OK. Please continue.

W: ...Summer Grove, CA, 08571.

M: OK, let me make sure I understand. You said "Summer Grove, California -California is abbreviated capital c capital a- is that correct?

W: Yes, that's correct.

M: And then 08571. Is that correct?

W: Yes, that's correct.

M: Could I have your telephone number?

W: Our telephone number is 595-238-2121.

M: OK, let me make sure I understand. You said that your telephone number is 595-238-2121. Is that correct?

W: Yes, that's correct.

M: How much were your company's annual sales?

W: Our annual sales were $121,814,384,273.

M: OK. Let me make sure I understand. You said that your annual sales were $121,814,384,273. Is that correct?

W: Yes, that's correct.

M: And how many employees does your company have?

W: Our company has 236,702 employees.

M: OK. Let me make sure I understand. You said your company has 236,702 employees. Is that correct?

W: Yes, that's correct.

Track 43 - Number 4

W: Who do you work for?

M: I work for Dark Cloud Financial Services.

W: Could you say that again?

M: Ah-huh. I work for Dark Cloud Financial Services.

W: Let me make sure I understand. You said you work for Dark Cloud Financial Services. Is that correct?

M: Yes, that's correct.

W: OK. Could I have your address?

M: Sure. Our address is One Dark Cloud Center, Miami, Florida 39264.

W: OK. Let me make sure I understand. You said your address is One Dark Cloud Center, Miami, Florida 39264. Is that correct?

M: Yes, that's correct.

W: And what is the abbreviation for Florida?

M: Florida is abbreviated capital f capital l.

W: Thank you. Could I have your telephone number?

M: Sure. Our telephone number is 497-206-3747.

W: OK. Let me make sure I understand. You said your telephone number is 497-206-3747. Is that correct?

M: Yes, that's correct.

W: OK. And how much were your annual sales?

M: Our annual sales were $38,657,748,275.

W: Let me make sure I understand. You said your annual sales were $38,657,748,275. Is that correct?

M: Yes, that's correct.

W: And how many employees does your company have?

M: Our company has 57,640 employees.

W: I'm sorry. Could you please say that again more clearly?

M: Ah-huh. Our company has 57,640 employees.

W: Let me make sure I understand. You said your company has 57,640 employees. Is that correct?

M: Yes, that's correct.

Track 44 - Skill 8: Take or leave a telephone message - Number 1

M: Hello. Geisert Corporation. This is Mark Smith.

W: Hello. This is Sandy Simpson from Brass Quarter Securities. Ah, may I speak to Tom Baker please?

M: I'm sorry. Tom Baker isn't here right now. Can I take a message?

W: Yes. Ah, could you ask him to call me back. My telephone number is 395-150-1567.

M: OK. Let me make sure I understand. Your telephone number is 395-150-1567. Is that correct?

W: Yes, that's correct.

M: And could I have your name again, please?

W: Yes, my name is Sandy Simpson.

M: Sandy is spelled capital s-a-n-d-y. Is that correct?

W: Yes, that's right.

M: And who do you work for?

W: I work for Brass Quarter Securities.

M: OK. I'm sorry. Did you say "Brass" - capital b-r-a-s-s?

Is that correct?

W: Yes that's correct.

M: OK. Let me make sure I understand. You said your name is Sandy Simpson, you work for Brass Quarter Securities, and your telephone number is area code 395-150-1567. Is that correct?

W: Yes, that's correct.

M: OK. I'll give him the message. Is there anything else I can do for you?

W: No that's everything. Thank you for your help.

M: It's my pleasure.

W: Good-bye.

M: Good-bye.

Track 45 - Number 2

W: Hello. Geisert Corporation. Mary Smith speaking.

M: Hello. Ah, this is Jeff Miller from Burlington Fenton Bank. Could I speak to Tom Baker please?

W: I'm sorry; Tom Baker isn't at his desk. Can I take a message?

M: Yeah. Could you ask him to call me back please? My telephone number is 996-408-5434.

W: OK. Let me make sure I understand. You said your telephone number is 996-408-5434. Is that correct?

M: Yes, that's correct.

W: OK. I'm sorry. Could I have your name again, please?

M: Ah-huh. My name is Jeff Miller.

W: And how do you spell Miller?

M: Miller is spelled capital m-i-l-l-e-r.

W: OK. Let me make sure I understand. You said Miller is spelled capital m-i-l-l-e-r. Is that correct?

M: Yes, that's correct.

W: And who do you work for?

M: I work for Burlington Fenton Bank.

W: OK. Ah, let me make sure I understand. You said you work for Burlington Fenton Bank.

M: Yes, that's correct.

W: OK. Ah, let me just make sure I understand. You want Mr. Baker to call you back. Your name is Jeff Miller, you work for Burlington Fenton Bank, and your phone number is 996-408-5434. Is that correct?

M: Yes, that's correct.

W: OK. I'll give him the message. Is there anything else I can do for you?

M: No that's everything. Thank you very much.

W: It's my pleasure.

M: Good-bye.

W: Good-bye.

Track 46 - Number 3

M: Hello. Geisert Corporation. Mark Smith speaking.

W: Hello. This is Kim Wrobel from Alpha Carp Incorporated. Ah, may I please speak to Tom Baker?

M: I'm sorry, Tom Baker is on vacation today.

W: Oh.

M: Would you like to leave a message?

W: Yes. Ah, could you ask him to call me back. My telephone number is 890-058-5605.

M: OK. Let me make sure I understand. You said your telephone number is 890-058-5605. Is that correct?

W: Yes, that's correct.

M: I'm sorry. Could I have your name again, please?

W: Sure. It's Kim Wrobel.

M: I'm sorry. How do you spell Wrobel?

W: Wrobel is spelled w-r-o-b-e-l. That's…

M: …OK, let me make sure I understand. You said Wrobel is spelled capital w-r-o-b-e-l. Is that correct.

W: Yes, that's correct.

M: And who do you work for again?

W: I work for Alpha Carp Incorporated.

M: Ah, I'm sorry. How do you spell Alpha?

W: Alpha is spelled capital a-l-p-h-a

M: OK. And how do you spell Carp?

W: Carp is spelled capital c-a-r-p.

M: OK. Let me make sure I understand. You said you work for Alpha Carp Incorporated. Alpha is spelled capital a-l-p-h-a and Carp is spelled capital c-a-r-p. Is that correct?

W: Yes, that's correct.

M: Incorporated.

W: Yes.

M: OK. I'll give him the message. Is there anything else I can do for you?

W: No that's everything. Thanks for your help.

M: It's my pleasure.

W: Good-bye.

M: Good-bye.

Track 47 - Number 4

W: Hello. Geisert Corporation. Mary Smith speaking.

M: Hello. This is Peter Holpuck with Moore Robins Finance. Could I speak to Tom Baker please?

W: I'm sorry, Tom Baker isn't in right now.

M: Mmmm. Ah, could you take a message?

W: Yes.

M: Could you ask him to call me back please? My telephone number is 697-465-4500.

W: OK. Let me make sure I understand. You said your phone number is 697-465-4500. Is that correct?

M: Yes, that's correct.

W: And, I'm sorry. Could I have your name again, please?

M: Ah-huh. My name is Peter Holpuck.

W: Peter Holpuck. How do you spell Holpuck?

M: Holpuck is spelled capital h-o-l-p-u-c-k.

W: Let me make sure I understand. You said Holpuck is spelled capital h-o-l-p-u-c-k. Is that correct?

M: Yes, that's correct.

W: And who do you work for?

M: I work for Moore Robin Finance.

W: OK. How do you spell Moore?

M: Moore is spelled capital m-o-o-r-e.

W: OK. So that's, let's see, you said "Moore is spelled capital m-o-o-r-e," and your company's name is Moore Robin Finance, is that correct?

M: Yes, that's correct.

W: OK, ah, let me just make sure I understand everything. Ah, you want Mr. Baker to call you back.

M: Mm-huh.

W: Your name is Peter Holpuck. Capital h-o-l-p-u-c-k. And you work for Moore Robin Finance. That's capital m-o-o-r-e Robin Finance. And your phone number is 697-465-4500. Is that correct?

M: Yes, that's correct.

W: OK. I'll give him the message. Is there anything else I can do for you?

M: No that's everything. Thank you for your help.

W: It's my pleasure.

M: Good-bye.

W: Good-bye.

Track 48 - Skill 11 – Making an appointment - Number 1

M: Do you like hamburgers?

W: Yes.

M: Great, let's go to McDonald's together.

W: OK.

M: What day shall we go?

W: Mmm, let's go on Monday.

M: OK. Where shall we meet?

W: Let's meet on the first floor.

M: What time shall we meet?

W: Ah, let's meet at 5 o'clock.

M: OK. Let me make sure I understand. I'll meet you on Monday, on the first floor at 5 o'clock. Is that correct?

W: Yes, that's correct.

M: OK, see you then.

W: See you then.

Track 49 - Number 2

W: Do you like shopping?

M: Yeah.

W: Great, let's go shopping together.

M: OK.

W: What day shall we go?

M: Ahh, let's go on Friday.

W: OK. Where shall we meet?

M: Mmmm. Ah, let's meet in front of the New York Stock Exchange.

W: OK. Ah, what time shall we meet?

M: Let's meet at, ah, 7:30 p.m.

W: All right. Let me make sure I understand. I'll meet you in front of the New York Stock Exchange, ah, at 7:30 p.m. on Friday. Is that correct?

M: Yes, that's correct.

W: OK, great, see you then.

M: See you then.

Track 50 - Number 3

M: Do you like coffee?

W: Yes.

M: Great, let's go to Starbucks.

W: OK.

M: What day shall we go?

W: Ah, let's go on Wednesday.

M: OK. What time shall we meet?

W: Let's meet at noon.

M: OK, and where shall we meet?

W: Ah, let's meet at Starbucks.

M: OK. Let me make sure I understand. I'll meet you at noon on Wednesday at Starbucks. Is that correct?

W: Yes, that's correct.

M: OK, see you then.

W: See you then.

Track 51 - Number 4

W: Do you like going to the movies?

M: Yeah.

W: Great, let's go to the movies together.

M: OK.

W: What day shall we go?

M: Um, let me see. Ah, Thursday.

W: OK. Where shall we meet?

M: Ah, let's meet in the hotel lobby.

W: OK. What time shall we meet?

M: Mm, let's meet at 6 p.m.

W: Let me make sure I understand. I'll meet you at 6 o'clock p.m. in the hotel lobby, on Thursday. Is that correct?

M: Yes, that's correct.

W: OK, see you then.

M: See you then.

Track 52 - Number 5

M: Do you like playing golf?
W: Yes.
M: Great, let's go play golf together.
W: OK.
M: What day shall we go?
W: Hmmm, let's go on Sunday.
M: OK. Ah, where shall we meet?
W: Let's meet, ah, in the golf course parking lot.
M: OK, what time shall we meet?
W: Let's meet at 7 o'clock a.m.
M: OK. Let me make sure I understand. I'll meet you on Sunday at 7 a.m. in the golf course parking lot. Is that correct?
W: Yes, that's correct.
M: OK, see you then.
W: See you then.

Track 53 - Number 6

W: Do you like bowling?
M: Yes.
W: Great, let's go bowling together.
M: OK.
W: What day shall we go?
M: Ummm, let me see. Ah, how about Saturday.
W: Where shall we meet?
M: Let's meet at the Seoul train station in front of the newspaper stand.
W: OK. And what time shall we meet?
M: Ah, let's meet at 11 o'clock a.m.
W: OK, let me make sure I understand. I'll meet you at the Seoul train station in front of the newspaper stand, on Saturday at 11 a.m. Is that correct?
M: Yes, that's correct.
W: Great. I'll see you then.
M: See you then.

Track 54 -
Skill 18 – Ask for, give and support an opinion - Number 1

M: Which do you think is better plastic or wood?
W: I think plastic is better than wood because plastic is cheaper
M: Let me make sure I understand. You think plastic is better than wood because plastic is cheaper. Is that correct?
W: Yes, that's correct.

Track 55 - Number 2

W: Which do you think is better flying to New York or taking the train?
M: I think flying to New York is better than taking the train because flying is faster.

W: Let me make sure I understand. You think flying to New York is better than taking the train because flying is faster. Is that correct?
M: Yes, that's correct.

Track 56 - Number 3

M: Which do you think is better increasing the price or lowering the quality?
W: Hmm. I think lowering the quality is better than increasing the price because customers prefer lower prices.
M: Let me make sure I understand, you think that lowering the quality is better than increasing the price because customers prefer lower prices. Is that correct?
W: Yes, that's correct.

Track 57 - Number 4

W: Which do you think is better hiring Mr. Smith, or hiring Mr. Jones.
M: I think that hiring Mr. Jones is better than hiring Mr. Smith. Eh, Mr. Smith lacks technical knowledge about our industry.
W: Let me make sure I understand. You think hiring Mr. Smith is better than hiring Mr. Jones because Mr. Jones lacks technical knowledge about our industry. Is that correct?
M: No, that isn't correct. I think hiring Mr. Jones is better than hiring Mr. Smith because Mr. Smith lacks technical knowledge about our industry.

Track 58 - Number 5

M: Which do you think is better firing three employees, or raising our prices?
W: Hmm. I think firing three employees is better than raising our prices because our products are already too expensive.
M: Let me make sure I understand. You think that firing three employees is better than raising our prices because our products are already too expensive. Is that correct?
W: Yes, that's correct.

Track 59 - Number 6

W: Which do you think is better promoting Ms. Douglas or promoting Ms. Parker?
M: Mm, let me see. I think promoting Ms. Parker is better than promoting Ms. Douglas, because Ms. Parker has contributed more to our company.
W: Let me make sure I understand. You think promoting Ms. Parker is better than promoting Ms. Douglas because Ms. Parker has contributed more to our company. Is that correct?
M: Yes, that's correct.